# The Consequences to Come
## American Power After Bush

edited by
## Robert B. Silvers
with Michael Shae

NEW YORK REVIEW BOOKS

*New York*

THIS IS A NEW YORK REVIEW BOOK

PUBLISHED BY THE NEW YORK REVIEW OF BOOKS

THE CONSEQUENCES TO COME:
AMERICAN POWER AFTER BUSH
edited by Robert B. Silvers with Michael Shae

This edition published in 2008
in the United States of America by
The New York Review of Books
435 Hudson Street
New York, NY 10014
www.nyrb.com

Library of Congress Cataloging-in-Publication Data

The consequences to come: American power after Bush / edited by Robert B. Silvers,
with Michael Shae.
    p. cm. — (New York Review books collections)
  ISBN-13: 978-1-59017-298-8 (alk. paper)
  ISBN-10: 1-59017-298-1 (alk. paper)
  1. United States—Politics and government—2001–   2. United States—Foreign relations—2001–   3. Bush, George W. (George Walker), 1946—Political and social views.
4. Cheney, Richard B.—Political and social views. 5. Bush, George W. (George Walker),
1946—influence. 6. Cheney, Richard B.—Influence. 7. Democratic Party (U.S.)
I. Silvers, Robert B. II. Shae, Michael.
E902.C659 2008
973.93—dc22

                                                                        2007049852

ISBN 978-1-59017-298-8
Printed in the United States of America on acid-free paper.
3 5 7 9 10 8 6 4 2

# The Consequences to Come
## American Power After Bush

# Contents

# Preface

MOST OF THE essays in this collection were published in *The New York Review* in 2007. This was the year, as Jonathan Freedland puts it in his article reprinted here, when a new consensus took hold

> that the 2003 invasion of Iraq was a calamity, that the presidency of George W. Bush has reduced America's standing in the world and made the US less, not more, secure.

These were conclusions that had been anticipated in many earlier essays in *The New York Review*, starting with Frances Fitzgerald's prescient article of September 2002, "George Bush and the World," written some nine months before the administration launched its Iraq war in March 2003. Drawing on talks with the older Bush's national security adviser Brent Scowcroft, she argued that President Bush was using the "huge domestic support [he] acquired on September 11" to pursue longstanding objectives, including "the overthrow of Saddam Hussein," which were then "newly justified as a part of the war on terrorism."

In fact, as she pointed out, for years before the Bush administration took office, Donald Rumsfeld and Paul Wolfowitz, among others, were calling for the overthrow of Saddam Hussein on grounds that he "posed a danger to the region, and in particular to Israel." And they and their long-standing ally Dick Cheney, as Scowcroft made clear, could count on the support of the President. As Joan Didion went on to show in her essay on Cheney published four years later, he soon became "the central player in the system of willed errors...that is the Bush administration." In retrospect, Scowcroft's willingness to make a public case against the younger Bush in this interview and in an Op-Ed piece in *The Wall Street Journal* in August 2002 was an act of desperation to prevent Iraq and the surrounding region from becoming, as he put it, a "cauldron" that would foster terrorism and cause damage to the US.

During and after the invasion, such contributors to the *Review* as Tim Judah, Christopher de Bellaigue, Max Rodenbeck, and Mark Danner reported in depth from Iraq and other parts of the Middle East on how one fantasy of the administration after the other collapsed during an occupation whose human and political consequences are still hardly comprehended—hundreds of thousands of dead and wounded, millions of refugees—while, as Peter Galbraith made clear in an article in *The New York Review* also reprinted here—the geopolitical influence of the Islamic Republic of Iran has been extended to an unprecedented degree.

The articles collected in this book describe some of these consequences, analyzing how they were concealed and how they gradually came to be recognized, in some cases, as Jonathan Raban and Frank Rich show, by ambitious young intellectuals who earlier had urged Bush on. If these essays share a perspective, it would be a determination both to reconstruct facts and to analyze hidden motives and failures. As Mark Danner shows, for example, Condoleezza Rice, on February 22, three weeks before the invasion, was able to give Bush and his guest, the president of Spain, what turned out to be a quite false account of the efforts of Hans Blix, the chief UN inspector, to find weapons of mass destruction in Iraq.

Blix had already told the Security Council, on February 14, that during the most recent phase of the inspections, "access to sites [in Iraq] has so far been without problems"; and he was soon to say, in his report to the Security Council of March 7, 2003, that the inspections should continue for a matter of months. In other words, as Frank Rich writes here, inspections would have "verified the truth: Saddam was bluffing, and his WMDs had been almost entirely destroyed in 1990." But according to the transcript from the meeting in Crawford, Texas, on February 22, published in Spain's *El País* and translated here, Rice said:

> We don't expect much from that report. As with the previous ones, it will be six of one and half a dozen of the other. I have the impression that Blix will now be more negative than before about the Iraqis' intentions.

The conversation at Crawford between Rice, Bush, and the evidently puzzled Spanish president should in retrospect be dismaying, but by now who will be surprised by it? According to several reports, the decision to invade Iraq had been made many months before, as Brent Scowcroft must have known. In the most recent account, by Jacob Weisberg in *The Bush Tragedy*, when Richard Haas, the State Department's director of policy planning, "went to present his case against the war to Condi Rice" on July 17, 2002, Rice "told him to save his breath—it was already a done deal." How are writers to deal with the resulting situation as it was described by Arthur Schlesinger Jr. in the last essay he wrote before he died, which is included here: "Vietnam was bad enough, but to repeat the same experiment thirty years later in Iraq is a strong argument for a case of national stupidity"?

In these writings our contributors were, in effect, diving into the wreckage of failed policies, trying to reconstruct the story of what happened with the kind of analytic research and skeptical commentary we were grateful to publish. Much about that story still remains obscure, including the full motives for the invasion. As Frank Rich, Michael Tomasky, and Mark Danner, among other contributors to this collection, suggest, no one should have any illusions that the damage to the US, to people in Iraq, and to the truth has been adequately assessed, or that the way is necessarily open to new directions.

—ROBERT B. SILVERS

# I

# CHENEY: THE FATAL TOUCH

## *Joan Didion*

IT WAS IN some ways predictable that the central player in the system of willed errors and reversals that is the Bush administration would turn out to be its vice-president, Richard B. Cheney. Here was a man with considerable practice in the reversal of his own errors. He was never a star. No one ever called him a natural. He reached public life with every reason to believe that he would continue to both court failure and overcome it, take the lemons he seemed determined to pick for himself and make the lemonade, then spill it, let someone else clean up. The son of two New Deal Democrats, his father a federal civil servant with the Soil Conservation Service in Casper, Wyoming, he more or less happened into a full scholarship to Yale: his high school girlfriend and later wife, Lynne Vincent, introduced him to her part-time employer, a Yale donor named Thomas Stroock who, he later told Nicholas Lemann, "called Yale and told 'em to take this guy." The beneficiary of the future Lynne Cheney's networking lasted three semesters, took a year off before risking a fourth, and was asked to leave.

"He was in with the freshman football players, whose major activity was playing cards and horsing around and talking a lot," his freshman roommate told the *Yale Daily News*, not exactly addressing the enigma. "Wasn't gonna go to college and buckle down" and "I didn't like the East" are two versions of how Cheney himself failed to address it. As an undergraduate at the University of Wyoming he interned with the Wyoming State Senate, which was, in a state dominated by cattle ranchers and oil producers and Union Pacific management, heavily Republican. This internship appears to have been when Cheney began identifying himself as a Republican. ("You can't take my vote for granted," his father would advise him when he first ran for Congress as a Republican.) He graduated from Wyoming in 1965 and, in the custom of the Vietnam years, went on to receive a master's degree. He never wrote a dissertation ("did all the work for my doctorate except the dissertation," as if the dissertation were not the point) and so never got the doctorate in political science for which he then enrolled at the University of Wisconsin.

Still, he persevered, or Lynne Cheney did. When, in 1968, at age twenty-seven, a no-longer-draft-eligible "academic" with a wife and a child and no Ph.D. and no clear clamor for his presence, he left Wisconsin for Washington, he managed to meet the already powerful Donald Rumsfeld about a fellowship in his House office. Cheney, by his own description and again failing to address the enigma, "flunked the interview." He retreated back to the only place at the table, the office of a freshman Republican Wisconsin congressman, Bill Steiger, for whom Cheney was said to be not a first choice and whose enthusiasm for increased environmental and workplace protections did not immediately suggest the Cheney who during his own ten years in Wyoming's single congressional seat would vote with metronomic regularity against any legislation tending in either direction.

The potential rewards of Washington appear to have mobilized Cheney as those of New Haven and Madison had not. Within the year, he was utilizing Steiger to make another move on Rumsfeld, who had been asked by Richard M. Nixon to join his new administration as director of the Office of Economic Opportunity. Cheney, James Mann wrote in *Rise of the Vulcans*, noticed a note on Steiger's desk from Rumsfeld, looking for advice and help in his new OEO job. Cheney spotted an opportunity. Over a weekend, he wrote an unsolicited memo for Steiger on how to staff and run a federal agency.

Rumsfeld hired Cheney, and, over the next few years, as he moved up in the Nixon administration, took Cheney with him. Again, in 1974, after the Nixon resignation, when Rumsfeld was asked to become Gerald Ford's chief of staff, he made Cheney his deputy.

In Cheney, Rumsfeld had found a right hand who took so little for granted that he would later, by the account of his daughter Mary, make a three-hour drive from Casper to Laramie to have coffee with three voters, two of whom had been in his wedding. In Rumsfeld, who would be described by Henry Kissinger as "a special Washington phenomenon: the skilled full-time politician-bureaucrat in whom ambition, ability, and substance fuse seamlessly," Cheney had found a model. In the Ford White House, where he and Rumsfeld were known as "the little Praetorians," Cheney cultivated a control of detail that extended even to questioning the use in the residence of "little dishes of salt with funny little spoons" rather than "regular salt shakers."

Together, Cheney and Rumsfeld contrived to marginalize Nelson Rockefeller as vice-president and edge him off the 1976 ticket. They convinced Ford that Kissinger was a political liability who should no longer serve as both secretary of state and national security adviser. They managed the replacement of William Colby as CIA chief with George H. W. Bush, a move interpreted by many as a way of rendering Bush unavailable to be Ford's running mate in 1976. They managed the replacement of James Schlesinger as secretary of defense with Rumsfeld himself. Cheney later described his role in such maneuvers as "the sand in the gears," the person who, for example, made sure that when Rockefeller was giving a speech the amplifier was turned down. In 1975, when Ford named Rumsfeld secretary of defense, it was Cheney, then thirty-four, who replaced Rumsfeld as chief of staff.

Relationships matter in public life, until they do not. In May 2006, during a commencement address at Louisiana State University, Cheney mentioned this long relationship with Rumsfeld by way of delivering the message that "gratitude, in general, is a good habit to get into":

> I think, for example, of the first time I met my friend and colleague Don Rumsfeld. It was back in the 1960s, when he was a congressman and I was interviewing for a fellowship on Capitol Hill. Congressman Rumsfeld agreed to talk to me, but things didn't go all that well....
>
> We didn't click that day, but a few years later it was Don Rumsfeld who noticed my work and offered me a position in the executive branch.

Note the modest elision ("it was Don Rumsfeld who noticed my work") of the speaker's own active role in these events. What Cheney wanted to stress that morning in Baton Rouge was not his own dogged tracking of the more glamorous Rumsfeld but the paths one had possibly "not expected to take," the "unexpected turns," the "opportunities that come suddenly and change one's plans overnight." The exact intention of these commencement remarks may be unknowable (a demonstration of loyalty? a warning? to whom? a marker to be called in later? all of the above?), but it did not seem accidental that they were delivered during a period when one four-star general, one three-star general, and four two-star generals were each issuing calls for Donald Rumsfeld's resignation as secretary of defense. Nor did it seem accidental that the President and the Vice President were taking equally stubborn and equally inexplicable lines on the matter of Rumsfeld's and by extension their own grasp on the war in Iraq. "I hear the voices and I read the front page and I know the speculation,"

George W. Bush said in response to a reporter's question during a Rose Garden event. "But I'm the decider and I decide what's best. And what's best is for Don Rumsfeld to remain as the secretary of defense."

The question of where the President gets the notions known to the nation as "I'm the decider" and within the White House as "the unitary executive theory" leads pretty fast to the blackout zone that is the Vice President and his office. It was the Vice President who took the early offensive on the contention that whatever the decider decides to do is by definition legal. "We believe, Jim, that we have all the legal authority we need," the Vice President told Jim Lehrer on PBS after it was reported that the National Security Agency was conducting warrantless wiretapping in violation of existing statutes. It was the Vice President who pioneered the tactic of not only declaring such apparently illegal activities legal but recasting them as points of pride, commands to enter attack mode, unflinching defenses of the American people by a president whose role as commander in chief authorizes him to go any extra undisclosed mile he chooses to go on their behalf.

"Bottom line is we've been very active and very aggressive defending the nation and using the tools at our disposal to do that," the Vice President advised reporters on a flight to Oman in December 2005. It was the Vice President who maintained that passage of Senator John McCain's legislation banning inhumane treatment of detainees would cost "thousands of lives." It was the Vice President's office, in the person of David S. Addington, that supervised the 2002 "torture memos," advising the President that the Geneva Conventions need not apply. And, after Admiral Stansfield Turner, director of the CIA between 1977 and 1981, referred to Cheney as "vice president for torture," it was the Vice President's office that issued this characteristically nonresponsive statement: "Our country is at war and our government has an obligation to protect the American people from a brutal enemy that has declared war upon us."

Addington, who emerged into government from Georgetown University and Duke Law School in 1981, the most febrile moment of the Reagan Revolution, is an instructive study in the focus Cheney favors in the protection of territory. As secretary of defense for George H.W. Bush, Cheney made Addington his special assistant and ultimately his general counsel. As vice-president for George W. Bush, Cheney again turned to Addington, and named him, after the indictment of I. Lewis "Scooter" Libby in connection with the exposure of Ambassador Joseph Wilson's wife as a CIA agent, his chief of staff. "You're giving away executive power," Addington has been reported to snap at less committed colleagues. He is said to keep a photograph in his office of Cheney firing a gun. He vets every line of the federal budget to eradicate any wording that might restrain the President. He also authors the "signing statements" now routinely issued to free the President of whatever restrictive intent might have been present in whichever piece of legislation he just signed into law. A typical signing statement, as written by Addington, will refer repeatedly to the "constitutional authority" of "the unitary executive branch," and will often mention multiple points in a single bill that the President declines to enforce.

Signing statements are not new, but at the time Bill Clinton left office, the device had been used, by the first forty-two presidents combined, fewer than six hundred times. George W. Bush, by contrast, issued more than eight hundred such takebacks during the first six years of his administration. Those who object to this or any other assumption of absolute executive power are reflexively said by those who speak for the Vice President to be "tying the president's hands," or "eroding his ability to do his job," or, more ominously, "aiding those who don't want him to do his job."

One aspect common to accounts of White House life is the way in which negative events tend to be interpreted as internal staffing failures, errors on the order of the little dishes of salt with the funny little spoons. Cheney did not take the lesson he might have taken from being in the White House at the time Saigon fell, which was that an administration can be overtaken by events that defeat the ameliorative power of adroit detail management. He took a more narrow lesson, the one that had to do with the inability of a White House to pursue victory if Congress "tied its hands." "It's interesting that [Cheney] became a member of Congress," former congressman Tom Downey said to Todd Purdum, "because I think he always thought we were a massive inconvenience to governing." Bruce Fein, who served in the Meese Justice Department during the Reagan administration, told Jane Mayer of *The New Yorker* that Cheney's absence of enthusiasm for checks and balances long predated any argument that this was a "wartime presidency" and so had special powers:

> This preceded 9/11. I'm not saying that warrantless surveillance did. But the idea of reducing Congress to a cipher was already in play. It was Cheney and Addington's political agenda.

"I have repeatedly seen an erosion of the powers and the ability of the president of the United States to do his job," the Vice President said after one year in office. "We are weaker today as an institution because of the unwise compromises that have been made over the last thirty to thirty-five years." "Watergate—a lot of the things around Watergate and Vietnam, both, in the '70s, served to erode the authority, I think, the President needs to be effective," he said to reporters accompanying him on that December 2005 flight to Oman. Expanding on this understanding of the separation of powers as a historical misunderstanding, the Vice President offered this:

> If you want reference to an obscure text, go look at the minority views that were filed with the Iran-Contra Committee; the Iran-Contra Report in about 1987. Nobody has ever read them, but we—part of the argument in Iran-Contra was whether or not

the President had the authority to do what was done in the Reagan years. And those of us in the minority wrote minority views, but they were actually authored by a guy working for me, for my staff, that I think are very good in laying out a robust view of the President's prerogatives with respect to the conduct of especially foreign policy and national security matters.

There are some recognizable Cheney touches here, resorts to the kind of self-deprecation (as in "I didn't like the East" and "I flunked the interview") that derives from a temperamental grandiosity. The "obscure text" that "nobody has ever read" was the two-hundred-page minority report included in the 1987 *Report of the Congressional Committees Investigating the Iran-Contra Affair*, a volume printed and widely distributed by the US Government Printing Office. The unidentified "guy working for me" was Addington, at the time of the Iran-contra hearings a counsel to the committees but during the events that led to Iran-contra an assistant general counsel at William Casey's CIA, where he would have been focused early on locating the legal enablement for what Theodore Draper, in his study of Iran-contra, *A Very Thin Line*, called the "usurpation of power by a small, strategically placed group within the government."

This minority report, which vehemently rejects not only the conclusions of the majority but even the report's ("supposedly 'factual'") narrative, does allow that "President Reagan and his staff made mistakes" during the course of Iran-contra. Yet the broadest mistake, the demented "arms for hostages" part of the scheme, the part where we deal the HAWK missiles to Iran through Manucher Ghorbanifar and Robert McFarlane flies to Tehran with the cake and the Bible and the falsified Irish passports, is strenuously defended as a "strategic opening," an attempt to "establish a new US relationship with Iran, thus strengthening the US strategic posture throughout the Persian Gulf region."

We had heard before, and have heard recently, about "strategic openings," "new relationships" that will reorder the Middle East. "Extremists in the region would have to rethink their strategy of Jihad," Cheney told the Veterans of Foreign Wars in August 2002 about the benefits that were to accrue from invading Iraq. "Moderates throughout the region would take heart. And our ability to advance the Israeli-Palestinian peace process would be enhanced, just as it was following the liberation of Kuwait in 1991." We had heard before, and have heard recently, that what might appear to be an administration run amok is actually an administration holding fast on constitutional principle.

Watergate, Cheney has long maintained, was not a criminal conspiracy but the result of a power struggle between the legislative and executive branches. So was the 1973 War Powers Act, which restricted executive authority to go to war without consulting Congress and which Cheney believed unconstitutional. So was the attempt to get Cheney to say which energy executives attended the 2001 meetings of his energy task force. This issue, both Cheney and Bush explained again and again, had nothing to do with Enron or the other energy players who might be expecting a seat at the table in return for their generous funding (just under $50 million) of the 2000 Republican campaign. "The issue that was involved there," Cheney said, misrepresenting what had been requested, which was not the content of the conversations but merely the names of those present, "was simply the question of whether or not a Vice President can sit down and talk with citizens and gain from them their best advice and counsel on how we might deal with a particular issue."

The 1987 minority report prefigures much else that has happened since. There is the acknowledgment of "mistakes" that turn out to be not exactly the mistakes we might have expected. The "mistake" in this administration's planning for the Iraq war, for example, derived not from having failed to do any planning but from arriving "too fast" in Baghdad, thereby losing the time, this scenario seemed to suggest, during which we had meant to think up a plan. Similarly, the "mistakes" in Iran-contra, as construed by the minority report, had followed not from having done the illegal but from having allowed the illegal to become illegal in the first place. As laid out by the minority, a principal "mistake" made by the Reagan administration in Iran-contra was in allowing President Reagan to sign rather than veto the 1984 Boland II Amendment forbidding aid to contra forces: no Boland II, no illegality. A second "mistake," to the same point, was Reagan's "less-than-robust defense of his office's constitutional powers, a mistake he repeated when he acceded too readily and too completely to waive executive privilege for our Committees' investigation."

The very survival of the executive species, then, was seen by Cheney and his people as dependent on its brute ability to claim absolute power and resist all attempts to share it. Given this imperative, the steps to our current situation had a leaden inevitability: if the executive branch needed a war to justify its claim to absolute power, then Iraq, Rumsfeld would be remembered to have said on September 12, 2001, had the targets. If the executive branch needed a story point to sell its war, then the Vice President would resurrect the aluminum tubes that not even the US Department of Energy believed to be meant for a centrifuge: "It's now public that, in fact, [Saddam] has been seeking to acquire...the kinds of tubes that are necessary to build a centrifuge." The Vice President would dismiss Joseph Wilson's report that he had found no yellowcake in Niger: "Did his wife send him on a junket?"

As for the weapons themselves, the Vice President would deride the collective judgment of his own intelligence community, which believed, according to Paul R. Pillar, then the CIA national intelligence officer for the Near East and South Asia, that any development of a nuclear weapon was several years away and would be best dealt with—given that the community's own analysis of the war option projected violent conflict between Sunnis and Shiites and guerrilla attacks on any occupying power—"through an aggressive inspections program to supplement the sanctions already in place." "Intelligence," the Vice President would say dismissively in an August 2002 speech to the Veterans of Foreign Wars, "is an uncertain business." The Vice President would override as irrelevant the facts that Hans Blix and his UN monitoring team were prepared to resume such inspections and in fact did resume them, conducting seven hundred inspections of five hundred sites, finding nothing but stopping only when the war intervened. "Simply stated, there is no doubt that Saddam Hussein now has weapons of mass destruction," he would declare in the same speech to the Veterans of Foreign Wars.

> A person would be right to question any suggestion that we should just get inspectors back into Iraq, and then our worries will be over.... A return of inspectors would provide no assurance whatsoever of [Saddam's] compliance with UN resolutions.

If the case for war lacked a link between September 11 and Iraq, the Vice President would repeatedly cite the meeting that neither American nor Czech intelligence believed had taken place between Mohamed Atta and Iraqi intelligence in Prague: "It's been pretty well confirmed that [Atta] did go to Prague and he did meet with a senior official of the Iraqi intelligence service in Czechoslovakia last April, several months before the attacks," he would say on NBC in December 2001. "We discovered...the allegation that one of the lead hijackers, Mohamed Atta, had, in fact, met with Iraqi intelligence in Prague," he would say on NBC in March 2002. "We have reporting that places [Atta] in Prague with a senior Iraqi intelligence officer a few months before the attacks on the World Trade Center," he would say on NBC in September 2002. "The senator has got his facts wrong," he would then say while debating Senator John Edwards during the 2004 campaign. "I have not suggested there's a connection between Iraq and 9/11."

This was not a slip of memory in the heat of debate. This was dishonest, a repeated misrepresentation, in the interests of claiming power, so bald and so systematic that the only instinctive response (*Did too!*) was that of the schoolyard. By June 2004, before the debate with Edwards, Cheney had in fact begun edging away from the Prague story, not exactly disclaiming it but characterizing it as still unproven, as in, on a Cincinnati TV station, "That's true. We do not have proof that there was such a connection." It would be two years later, March 2006, before he found it prudent to issue a less equivocal, although still shifty, version. "We had one report early on from another intelligence service that suggested that the lead hijacker, Mohamed Atta, had met with Iraqi intelligence officials in Prague, Czechoslovakia," he told Tony Snow on Fox News. "And that reporting waxed and waned where the degree of confidence in it, and so forth, has been pretty well knocked down at this stage, that that meeting ever took place. So we've never made the case, or argued the case, that somehow [Saddam Hussein] was directly involved in 9/11. That evidence has never been forthcoming."

What the Vice President was doing with the intelligence he received has since been characterized as "cherry-picking," a phrase suggesting that he selectively used only the more useful of equally valid pieces of intelligence. This fails to reflect the situation. The White House had been told by the CIA that no meeting in Prague between Mohamed Atta and Iraqi intelligence had ever occurred. The International Atomic Energy Agency and the US Department of Energy had said that the aluminum tubes in question "were not directly suitable" for uranium enrichment. The White House had been told by the CIA that the British report about Saddam Hussein attempting to buy yellowcake in Nigeria was doubtful.

"The British government has learned that Saddam Hussein recently

sought significant quantities of uranium from Africa," the President
nonetheless declared in his 2003 State of the Union address, the "sixteen enormously overblown words" for which Condoleezza Rice
would blame the CIA and for which George Tenet, outplayed, would
take the hit. Nor would the President stop there: "Our intelligence
sources tell us that he has attempted to purchase high-strength aluminum tubes suitable for nuclear weapons production."

What the Vice President was doing, then, was not cherry-picking
the intelligence but rejecting it, replacing it with whatever self-
interested rumor better advanced his narrative line. "Cheney's office
claimed to have sources," Ron Suskind was told by those to whom he
spoke for *The One Percent Doctrine.*

> And Rumsfeld's, too. They kept throwing them [at the CIA]. The
> same information, five different ways. They'd omit that a key
> piece had been discounted, that the source had recanted. Sorry,
> our mistake. Then it would reappear, again, in a memo the next
> week.

The Vice President would not then or later tolerate any suggestion
that the story he was building might rest on cooked evidence. In a single speech at the American Enterprise Institute in November 2005
he used the following adjectives to describe those members of Congress who had raised such a question: "corrupt," "shameless," "dishonest," "reprehensible," "irresponsible," "insidious," and "utterly
false." "It's not about our analysis, or finding a preponderance of evidence," he is reported by Suskind to have said in the November 2001
briefing during which he articulated the doctrine that if there was "a
one percent chance" of truth in any suspicion or allegation, it must be
considered true. "It's about our response."

To what end the story was being cooked was hard to know. The
Vice President is frequently described as "ideological," or "strongly

conservative," but little in his history suggests the intellectual commitment implicit in either. He made common cause through the run-up to Iraq with the neoconservative ideologues who had burrowed into think tanks during the Clinton years and resurfaced in 2001 in the departments of State and Defense and the White House itself, but the alliance appeared even then to be more strategic than felt. The fact that Paul Wolfowitz and Richard Perle and Elliott Abrams shared with Cheney a wish to go to war in Iraq could create, in its confluence with September 11, what many came to call a perfect storm—as if it had blown up out of the blue beyond reach of human intervention—but the perfect storm did not make Cheney a neocon.

He identifies himself as a conservative, both political and cultural. He presents himself as can-do, rock-solid even if he is forced to live in Washington (you know he only does it on our behalf), one politician who can be trusted not to stray far from whatever unexamined views were current in the intermountain West during the 1950s and 1960s. He has described a 1969 return visit to the University of Wisconsin, during which he took Bill Steiger and George H. W. Bush to an SDS rally, as having triggered his disgust with the Vietnam protest movement. "We were the only guys in the hall wearing suits that night," he told Nicholas Lemann. As a congressman he cast votes that reflected the interests of an energy-driven state that has voted Republican in every presidential election but one since 1952. His votes in the House during 1988, the last year he served there, gave him an American Conservative Union rating of 100.

Yet his move to push Nelson Rockefeller off Gerald Ford's 1976 ticket had seemed based less on philosophical differences than on a perception of Rockefeller as in the way, in the lights, a star, like Kissinger, who threatened the power Cheney and Rumsfeld wielded in the Ford White House. In 1976, unlike most who called themselves conservatives, Cheney remained untempted by Reagan and clung to Ford, his best ticket to ride. Nor did he initially back Reagan in 1980.

Nor, when it has not been in his interest to do so, has he since taken consistent positions on what would seem to be his own most hardened policies.

"I think it is a false dichotomy to be told that we have to choose between 'commercial' interests and other interests that the United States might have in a particular country or region around the world," he said at the Cato Institute in 1998, during the period he was CEO of Halliburton, after he had pursued one war against Iraq and before he would pursue the second. He was arguing against the imposition by the United States of unilateral economic sanctions on such countries as Libya and Iran, two countries, although he did not mention this, in which Halliburton subsidiaries had been doing business. Nor did he mention, when he said in the same speech that he thought multilateral sanctions "appropriate" in the case of Iraq, that Iraq was a third country in which a Halliburton subsidiary would by the year's end be doing business.

The notion that he takes a consistent view of America's role in the world nonetheless remains general. The model on which he has preferred to operate is the cold war, or, to use the words in which he and the President have repeatedly described the central enterprise of their own administration, the "different kind of war," the war in which "our goal will not be achieved overnight." He has mentioned H. Bradford Westerfield, a political scientist at Yale and at the time Cheney took his introductory course a self-described hawk, as someone who influenced his thinking, but Westerfield later told the *Nation* correspondent John Nichols that his own hard line had softened by late 1967 or early 1968, when he came to see that Vietnam "really was unwinnable" and "the hawkish view was unrealistic."

Cheney, by then positioning himself in Washington, never drew those conclusions, nor, when he saw Westerfield in the 1990s at a memorial service for Les Aspin, did he seem to Westerfield interested in discussing them. "He seems to be determined to go his own way, no matter what facts he is confronted with," Westerfield told Nichols. "As a veteran of the political wars," Henry Kissinger later wrote about the years when Saigon was falling and Donald Rumsfeld and Richard Cheney were running the Ford White House,

> Rumsfeld understood far better than I that Watergate and Vietnam were likely to evoke a conservative backlash and that what looked like a liberal tide after the election of the McGovernite Congress in fact marked the radical apogee.

Rumsfeld and Cheney, in other words, had transcended what others might present as facts. They could feel the current. They knew how to catch the wave and ride it.

Cheney leaves no paper trail. He has not always felt the necessity to discuss what he plans to say in public with the usual offices, including that of the President. Nor, we learned from Ron Suskind, has he always felt the necessity, say if the Saudis send information to the President in preparation for a meeting, to bother sending that information on to Bush. Only on the evening of September 11, 2001, did it occur to Richard A. Clarke that in his role as national security coordinator he had briefed Cheney on terrorism and also Condoleezza Rice and Colin Powell, but never the President. Since November 1, 2001, under this administration's Executive Order 13233, which limits access to all presidential and vice-presidential papers, Cheney has been the first vice-president in American history entitled to executive privilege, a claim to co-presidency reinforced in March 2003 by Executive Order 13292, giving him the same power to classify information as the president has.

He runs an office so disinclined to communicate that it routinely refuses to disclose who works there, even for updates to the *Federal Directory*, which lists names and contact addresses for government officials. "We just don't give out that kind of information," an aide told one reporter. "It's just not something we talk about." When he visits his house in Jackson Hole and the local paper spots his plane and the anti-missile battery that accompanies him, the office until recently refused to confirm his presence: "In the past, they've been kind of weird," the paper's co-editor told *The Washington Post* in August 2006. "They'd say, 'His airplane's here and the missile base is here, but we can't tell you if he's here.'"

His every instinct is to withhold information, hide, let surrogates speak for him, as he did after the quail-shooting accident on the Armstrong ranch. His own official spoken remarks so defy syntactical analysis as to suggest that his only intention in speaking is to further obscure what he thinks. Possibly the most well-remembered statement he ever made (after "Big-time") was that he did not serve in the Vietnam War because he had "other priorities." Bob Woodward, in *Plan of Attack*, describes an exchange that took place between Cheney and Colin Powell in September 2002, when Cheney was determined that the US not ask the UN for the resolution against Iraq that the Security Council, after much effort by Powell, passed in November:

> Powell attempted to summarize the consequences of unilateral action.... He added a new dimension, saying that the international reaction would be so negative that he would have to close American embassies around the world if we went to war alone.
>
> That is not the issue, Cheney said. Saddam and the clear threat is the issue.
>
> Maybe it would not turn out as the vice president thinks, Powell said. War could trigger all kinds of unanticipated and unintended consequences....
>
> Not the issue, Cheney said.

In other words the Vice President had by then passed that point at which going to war was "not about our analysis." He had passed that point at which going to war was not about "finding a preponderance of evidence." At the point he had reached by September 2002, going to war was not even about the consequences. Not the issue, he had said. The personality that springs to mind is that of the ninth-grade bully in the junior high lunchroom, the one sprawled in the letter jacket so the seventh-graders must step over his feet. There was in a June 2006 letter from Senator Arlen Specter to Cheney, made public by Specter, an image that eerily conveyed just that: "I was surprised, to say the least, that you sought to influence, really determine, the action of the Committee without calling me first, or at least calling me at some point," Specter wrote, referring to actions Cheney had taken to block his Judiciary Committee from conducting a hearing on NSA surveillance. "This was especially perplexing since we both attended the Republican Senators caucus lunch yesterday and I walked directly in front of you on at least two occasions enroute from the buffet to my table."

There was a reason, beyond the thrill of their sheer arrogance, why the words "other priorities" stuck in the national memory. They were first uttered not in but outside the room in which Cheney's 1989 confirmation hearings were held, to a *Washington Post* reporter who asked why the candidate for secretary of defense had sought the five (four student and one "hardship") deferments that had prevented him from serving in Vietnam. This is what the candidate said:

> I had other priorities in the '60s than military service. I don't regret the decisions I made. I complied fully with all the requirements of the statutes, registered with the draft when I turned 18. Had I been drafted, I would have been happy to serve. I think those who did in fact serve deserve to be honored for their service.... Was it a noble cause? Yes, indeed, I think it was.

The words stuck because they resonated, and still do. They resonated the same way the words "fixed himself a cocktail back at the house" resonated when Katharine Armstrong, Cheney's hostess and fill-in (in the vacuum of his silence) apologist, used them to explain what he had done after the quail-hunting accident in lieu of either going to the hospital with Harry Whittington or explaining to the sheriff's office how he had just shot him. "Fixed himself a cocktail back at the house" suggested the indifference to assuming responsibility for his own mistakes that had become so noticeable in his public career. "Ultimately, I am the guy who pulled the trigger and fired the round that hit Harry," he managed, four days later, to say to Fox News in a memorable performance of a man accepting responsibility but not quite. "You can talk about all the other conditions that existed at the time, but that's the bottom line. It's not Harry's fault. You can't blame anybody else."

Like "it's not Harry's fault," which implied that you or I or any other fair observer (for example Katharine Armstrong, characterized by Cheney as "an acknowledged expert in all of this") might well conclude that it had been, "other priorities" suggested a familiar character wrinkle, in this case the same willingness to cloud an actual issue with circular arguments ("I complied fully with all the requirements of the statutes") that would later be demonstrated by the Vice President's people when they maintained that the Geneva Conventions need not apply to Afghan detainees because Afghanistan was a "failed state." What these tortured and in many cases invented legalities are designed to preclude is any acknowledgment that the issue at hand, whether it is avoiding military service or authorizing torture, might have a moral or an ethical or even a self-interested dimension that merits discussion.

This latter dimension, self-interest, which was the basis for John McCain's argument that we could not expect others to honor the Geneva Conventions if we did not do so ourselves, was dismissed by David Addington, at the time Cheney's legal architect, in the "new paradigm" memo he drafted in 2002 to go to the President over

White House Counsel Alberto R. Gonzales's signature. "It should be noted that your policy of providing humane treatment to enemy detainees gives us the credibility to insist on like treatment for our soldiers," the memo read, sliding past a key point, which was that the "new paradigm" differentiated between "enemy detainees" and "illegal enemy combatants," or "terrorists," a distinction to be determined by whoever did the detaining.

> Moreover, even if GPW [Geneva Convention III Relative to the Treatment of Prisoners of War] is not applicable, we can still bring war crimes charges against anyone who mistreats US personnel. Finally, I note that . . . terrorists will not follow GPW rules in any event.

This is not law. This is casuistry, the detritus of another perfect storm, the one that occurred when the deferments of the Vietnam years met the ardor of the Reagan Revolution.

About this matter of priorities. At an October 2005 meeting at Stanford University of the American Academy of Arts and Sciences, the historian David M. Kennedy expressed concern about the absence of political accountability in a nation where

> no American is now obligated to military service, few will ever serve in uniform, even fewer will actually taste battle—and fewer still of those who do serve will have ever sat in the classrooms of an elite university like Stanford. . . . Americans with no risk whatsoever of exposure to military service have, in effect, hired some of the least advantaged of their fellow countrymen to do some of their most dangerous business while the majority goes on with their own affairs unbloodied and undistracted.

Early in 1995, his tenure as George H. W. Bush's secretary of defense timed out, Dick Cheney was raising money for a stalled 1996 presidential run when he was asked, legendarily out of the blue on a fly-fishing trip but in fact unsurprisingly for someone with government connections in both energy and defense, to become CEO of Halliburton. In the early summer of 2000, flying home with his daughter Mary from a hunting trip, Cheney, then five years into his job at Halliburton, a period for which he had collected $44 million (plus deferments and stock options) and during which the Halliburton subsidiary Brown & Root had billed the United States $2 billion for services in Bosnia and Kosovo, told Mary that Joe Allbaugh, the national campaign manager of George W. Bush's 2000 campaign, had asked him to consider being Bush's running mate. In July 2000, after conducting a search for another candidate and detailing the reasons why he himself would be a bad choice ("Knowing my dad, I'm sure he didn't hold anything back as he laid out the disadvantages of selecting him as the nominee"), in other words assuring himself carte blanche, Cheney agreed to join the ticket.

In February 2001, Joe Allbaugh, whose previous experience was running the governor's office for Bush in Texas, became head of FEMA, where he hired Michael D. ("Brownie, you're doing a heckuva job") Brown. In December 2002, Allbaugh announced that he was resigning from FEMA, leaving Brown in charge while he himself founded New Bridge Strategies, LLC, "a unique company," according to its Web site, "that was created specifically with the aim of assisting clients to evaluate and take advantage of business opportunities in the Middle East following the conclusion of the US-led war in Iraq."

This was the US-led war in Iraq that had not then yet begun. When David Kennedy spoke at Stanford about the vacuum in political accountability that could result from waging a war while a majority of Americans went on "with their own affairs unbloodied and undistracted," he was talking only about the absence of a draft. He was not talking about the ultimate step, the temptation to wage the war itself

to further private ends, or "business opportunities," or other priorities. Nor was he talking about the intermediate step, which was to
replace the manpower no longer available by draft by contracting out
"logistical" support to the private sector, in other words by privatiz-
ing the waging of the war. This step, now so well known as to be a
plot point on *Law and Order* (civilian contract employees in Iraq fall
out among themselves; a death ensues; Sam Waterston sorts it out),
had already been taken. There are now, split among more than 150
private firms, thousands of such contracts outstanding. Halliburton
alone had by July 2004 contracts worth $11,431,000,000.

Private firms in Iraq have done more than build bases and bridges
and prisons. They have done more than handle meals and laundry
and transportation. They train Iraqi forces. They manage security.
They interrogate prisoners. Contract interrogators from two firms,
CACI International (according to its Web site "a world leader in providing timely solutions to the intelligence community") and Titan ("a
leading provider of comprehensive information and communications
products, solutions, and services for National Security"), were accused
of abuses at Abu Ghraib, where almost half of all interrogators and
analysts were CACI employees. They operate free of oversight. They
distance the process of interrogation from the citizens in whose name,
or in whose "defense," or to ensure whose "security," the interrogation is being conducted. They offer "timely solutions."

In his 1991 book *A Very Thin Line*, Theodore Draper wrote:

> The Iran-contra affairs amounted to more than good plans gone
> wrong or even bad plans gone wildly wrong. They were symp-
> tomatic of a far deeper disorder in the American body politic.
> They were made possible by an interpretation of the Constitu-
> tion which Poindexter and North thought gave them a license to
> carry on their secret operations in the name of the president, in
> defiance of the law and without the knowledge of any other

branch of government. . . . Somehow the highly dubious theory
of a presidential monopoly of foreign policy had filtered down
to them and given them a license to act as if they could substi-
tute themselves for the entire government.

There remains a further reason why "other priorities" still nags. It
suggests other agendas, undisclosed strategies. We had watched this
White House effect the regulatory changes that would systematically
dismantle consumer and workplace and environmental protections.
We had watched this White House run up the deficits that ensured
that the conservative dream of rolling back government will necessarily take place, because there will be no money left to pay for it. We
had heard the Vice President speak as recently as January 2004 about
our need to recolonize the world, build bases, "warm bases, bases we
can fall in on, on a crisis and have present the capabilities we need to
operate from." "Other priorities" suggests what the Vice President
might have meant when he and the President talked about the "different kind of war," the war in which "our goal will not be achieved
overnight." As a member of the House during the cold war and then
as secretary of defense during the Gulf War and then as CEO of Halliburton, the Vice President had seen up close the way in which a war
in which "our goal will not be achieved overnight" could facilitate
the flow of assets from the government to the private sector and back
to whoever in Washington greases the valves. "The first person to
greet our soldiers as they arrive in the Balkans and the last one to
wave goodbye is one of our employees," as he put it during his Halliburton period.

He had also seen up close the political advantage to which such a
war could be put. "And so if there's a backlash pending I think the
backlash is going to be against those who are suggesting somehow
that we shouldn't take these steps in order to protect the country," as he
put it when asked in December 2005 if his assumption of presidential

autonomy might not provoke a congressional backlash. In the apparently higher interest of consolidating that political advantage he had made misrepresentations that facilitated a war that promised to further destabilize the Middle East. He had compromised both America's image in the world and its image of itself. In 1991, explaining why he agreed with George H.W. Bush's decision not to take the Gulf War to Baghdad, Cheney had acknowledged the probability that any such invasion would be followed by civil war in Iraq:

> Once you've got Baghdad, it's not clear what you do with it. It's not clear what kind of government you would put in.... Is it going to be a Shia regime, a Sunni regime or a Kurdish regime? Or one that tilts toward the Baathists, or one that tilts toward the Islamic fundamentalists?... How long does the United States military have to stay to protect the people that sign on for that government, and what happens to it once we leave?

By January 2006, when the prescience of these questions was evident and polling showed that 47 percent of Iraqis approved of "attacks on US-led forces," and the administration was still calculating that it could silence domestic doubt by accusing the doubter of wanting to "cut and run," the Vice President assured Fox News that the course had been true. "When we look back on this ten years hence," he said, a time frame suggesting that he was once again leaving the cleanup to someone else, "we will have fundamentally changed the course of history in that part of the world, and that will be an enormous advantage for the United States and for all of those countries that live in the region."

—September 7, 2006

## BIBLIOGRAPHY

Blix, Hans. *Disarming Iraq*. Pantheon, 2004.

Bremer, L. Paul III, with Malcolm McConnell. *My Year in Iraq: The Struggle to Build a Future of Hope*. Simon and Schuster, 2006.

Briody, Dan. *The Halliburton Agenda: The Politics of Oil and Money*. Wiley, 2004.

Cheney, Mary. *Now It's My Turn: A Daughter's Chronicle of Political Life*. Threshold, 2006.

Clarke, Richard. *Against All Enemies: Inside America's War on Terror*. Free Press, 2004.

Danner, Mark. *Torture and Truth: America, Abu Ghraib, and the War on Terror*. New York Review Books, 2004.

Dean, John. *Worse Than Watergate: The Secret Presidency of George W. Bush*. Little, Brown, 2004.

Draper, Theodore. *A Very Thin Line: The Iran-Contra Affairs*. Hill and Wang, 1991.

Kissinger, Henry. *Years of Renewal*. Simon and Schuster, 1999.

Mann, James. *Rise of the Vulcans: The History of Bush's War Cabinet*. Viking, 2004.

Nichols, John. *The Rise and Rise of Richard B. Cheney: Unlocking the Mysteries of the Most Powerful Vice President in American History*. New Press, 2005.

*Report of the Congressional Committees Investigating the Iran-Contra Affair, with Supplemental, Minority, and Additional Views*. Government Printing Office, 1987.

Suskind, Ron. *The One Percent Doctrine: Deep Inside America's Pursuit of Its Enemies Since 9/11*. Simon and Schuster, 2006.

Turner, Admiral Stansfield. *Burn Before Reading: Presidents, CIA Directors, and Secret Intelligence*. Hyperion, 2005.

Werth, Barry. *31 Days: The Crisis That Gave Us the Government We Have Today*. Nan A. Talese/Doubleday, 2006.

Woodward, Bob. *Plan of Attack*. Simon and Schuster, 2004.

# 2

# NO EXIT

## *Joseph Lelyveld*

THE BUSH ADMINISTRATION seems never to have put it quite so baldly but in its rush to consolidate its authority after the terrorist attacks of September 11, it came close to asserting the power of the commander in chief to declare anyone in the world, of whatever citizenship or location, "an unlawful enemy combatant" and—solely on the basis of that designation—to detain the person indefinitely without charge, beyond reach of any court. As we now know, it then acted on its own theory; according to a list being compiled by Human Rights Watch, alleged terrorists were detained at American behest in Mauritania, Bosnia, Indonesia, the United Arab Emirates, and Yemen—as well as Afghanistan and the border areas of Pakistan where most al-Qaeda and Taliban fighters were captured. Many of them were then turned over to the United States for transfer to the prison hastily constructed out of cargo containers in the American military enclave at Guantánamo, or other overseas detention centers used by the United States.[1]

---

1. The sense that normal legal restraints had been suspended showed up elsewhere. Italian magistrates charged agents of the Central Intelligence Agency in a kidnapping on the streets of Milan. In that case, "extraordinary rendition" to Egypt of the captured man appears to have obviated any need for him to be declared a combatant. (Also on renditions, see Raymond Bonner, "The CIA's Secret Torture," *The New York Review*, January 11, 2007.)

The five years since the first shackled prisoners were unloaded at Guantánamo have not been uneventful for constitutional scholars, lawyers concerned with human rights, and journalists of an investigative bent. Their questions and discovery motions have shaken loose information, including the names of many detainees, out of a government committed to secrecy. That information has been used as kindling for a slow-burning debate on coercive interrogation that eventually led Congress—nearly two years after publication of the notorious pictures of naked Iraqis stacked and taunted at Abu Ghraib prison—to affirm legislatively in the Detainee Treatment Act of 2005 that existing laws and treaty commitments barring torture and cruel, inhuman, and degrading treatment (sometimes called "torture lite") were still binding on American interrogators in what was grandiosely called "the Global War on Terror."

At least the question of cruel, inhuman, and degrading treatment had been addressed; how effectively is another matter. The Supreme Court has also cautiously asserted its jurisdiction on detention issues, picking apart arguments made on behalf of an executive branch that hubristically called on the Court to stand aside and, essentially, let the President reign. But—as the remaining 395 captives at Guantánamo enter the sixth year of their imprisonment without a single one of them having been put on trial—the question of whether we're prepared to hold terrorist suspects without charge for the rest of their natural lives has yet to be squarely addressed by either Congress or the courts. Decisions on detention issues have been handed down and laws have been passed. Some of these may now be revisited by the incoming Democratic Congress—in particular, the Military Commissions Act of 2006, which, among other things, denies non-US citizens who have been arrested and held in prison recourse to the writ of habeas corpus. But the question of indefinite detention itself—which might be construed as a core issue—hangs over our discussions like a far-off thundercloud, darkening a little with each passing year and each report of another suicide attempt at Guantánamo. From the standpoint of the detainees, nothing much has changed over the years.

The argument that putative combatants—would-be combatants who have merely been trained as well as those picked up in the vicinity of a battlefield—can be held in wartime until the end of hostilities isn't in itself novel or controversial. What's new in the current conflict, as it pertains to al-Qaeda and those detainees who are alleged to be its followers, is that no one can imagine the armistice or surrender that would signify an end to this war. In these circumstances, or so it now seems, indefinite could prove to be synonymous with endless; in effect, it could signify a life sentence. This would be a far cry from the preventive detention imagined as appropriate in a conventional war by the authors of the Geneva Conventions, which were intended as a rulebook ensuring humane treatment on all sides of those imprisoned for the specific purpose of keeping them out of military action. What has been at issue are the questions of whether the United States has legally been in a state of war since September 19, 2001, when Congress authorized the use of military force against those responsible for the attacks a week earlier, and if it has been, where that war begins and ends.

Also at issue, obviously, is whether—assuming we're in a war that's even bigger than the ones US troops have been committed to in Afghanistan and Iraq—the President is constitutionally entitled to unilaterally make up new rules and procedures for the treatment of captured supporters of terrorist movements. Since 2001, the United States has tended to cite those parts of international law that serve its purpose and shrug off, dispute, or discount others. "Customary laws of war," the government has correctly argued, justify holding prisoners indefinitely without charge. At the same time, it has contended that the Geneva Conventions, the modern codification of "the customary laws of war," don't apply because al-Qaeda and its offshoots are not parties to them and, all too obviously, have no regard for their standards.

Terrorists who dispatch suicide bombers and behead hostages obviously don't concern themselves with the welfare of civilians and prisoners, so there is little or no prospect of the reciprocity the Geneva regime encourages in conflicts between nations. But the conduct of al-Qaeda and its cohorts hardly relieves the United States of its responsibility to comply with the Geneva standards. The irony is that only the Geneva provisions on prisoners of war—a formal status denied the supposed terrorists the US has detained since 2001—provide a firm legal basis for indefinite detention without charge. According to the Geneva Conventions, those who are suspected of having committed terrorist acts can be charged criminally in front of a military or civil court; but the preventive detention of Islamic militants on the basis of a prudent or cockeyed suspicion that they may harbor terrorist ambitions is harder to justify in terms of existing international law or the US Constitution, which reserves to Congress the power to suspend the writ of habeas corpus in exceptional circumstances only: "when in cases of rebellion or invasion the public safety may require it."

The outgoing Republican Congress effectively did just that as far as detained aliens, designated as "illegal enemy combatants"—or indeed any aliens—were concerned when it passed the Military Commissions Act of 2006 in the run-up to the election campaign, in hopes of making an issue of Democratic "nay" votes.[2] That political tactic failed but the law is on the books. Now that Democrats have narrow control of the Senate Judiciary Committee, its new chairman, Senator Patrick J. Leahy, hopes to overturn what he has called "this sickening

---

2. According to a statement signed by some thirty constitutional scholars, the implication of the government's position is that any foreigner living legally in the United States can be held indefinitely without charge once classified as an "illegal enemy combatant" by the president. The scholars were reacting to the case of Ali al-Marri, a citizen of Qatar, who was arrested in Illinois and has been held in solitary confinement since 2001 at the Navy brig in Charleston, South Carolina, where his family has been denied the right to visit him. See Adam Liptak, "In War with Vague Boundaries, Detainee Longs for Court," *The New York Times*, January 5, 2007.

habeas provision." Even if he is successful, there are still likely to be roughly 250 prisoners at Guantánamo alone facing indefinite detention without charge. A more carefully written law may make it possible for some among them, in the fullness of time, to challenge their designation as "illegal enemy combatants" and their imprisonment. But so far there has been no sign that Democrats care to wrestle with the premise that it's legitimate to hold prisoners indefinitely without charge and to leave them to await the end of a war that shows no sign of ending. Staff aides dealing with detention matters say the Democrats are concentrating on "process issues"—restoring habeas corpus or whether the Uniform Code of Military Justice should govern the handling of evidence before military commissions—rather than the fate of individual prisoners.

The debate over detention issues—and action in the courts—has focused on Guantánamo but the Cuban outpost is only the most exposed of our prisons in this "war on terror." The census and status of the more remote prisons is murkier but US forces also hold prisoners in Iraq and at the air force base at Bagram in Afghanistan.[3] It's possible that there are still other prisons borrowed from other governments that have yet to be uncovered or acknowledged. President Bush conceded in September 2006 that the Central Intelligence Agency did in fact maintain such prisons abroad; he said they weren't being used at that moment but would be held in reserve. The striking decline of the prison population at Guantánamo in the last year or so—resulting from an effort to repatriate prisoners reclassified as NLECS (for "no longer enemy combatants")—points to a possibility that still other facilities may have been found; either that or the government has arrived at a recognition that the United States cannot conceivably detain every

---

3. Administration lawyers have cited a United Nations Security Council resolution recognizing the United States as an occupying authority in Iraq, passed after the start of the occupation, as a legal basis for the US continuing to hold security detainees in what's now considered to be a sovereign Iraq.

would-be Islamic fighter in a world where new ones are appearing daily on the streets of Baghdad or in the frontier towns of Pakistan.

The number of prisoners at Camp Delta, as the prison at Guantánamo was officially named, was expected to exceed 2,000 in early Pentagon projections; in late 2002, it topped out at slightly more than 650. By late 2006, the Guantánamo census had declined to 395; an estimated 14,500 were being held at various Iraq locations and about 500 at Bagram. How many of the prisoners in Iraq and Afghanistan have been held for a period of years—and may continue to be held indefinitely—without charge is uncertain; how many are non-Iraqi and non-Afghan is also a matter of guesswork for those who don't have access to classified information. (The organization Human Rights First, relying on official US figures, estimates that between 60,000 and 70,000 persons have been detained around the globe at one time or another by the United States since the first frantic efforts in 2001 to sweep up as many likely agents and contacts of terrorist networks as possible. The total ought to include the more than one thousand aliens, mostly Muslim, held in the United States after the September 11 attacks, on unrelated immigration charges or as so-called "material witnesses," on orders of Attorney General John Ashcroft.)

In all, more than 250 Guantánamo prisoners have been repatriated. In some cases, their release appears to have had more to do with diplomatic pressure applied by allied countries in which they had legal residence than with the facts of their particular cases. Prisoners with residence in European countries predominated in the early releases. In other cases—by now, most of them—the releases can be reasonably read as a tacit acknowledgment that they were no longer a serious threat nor of any significant value from an intelligence standpoint and probably never had been. The State Department is seeking to negotiate the release of about eighty-five Guantánamo prisoners to foreign countries but is running into difficulties getting foreign governments to agree to American conditions for continued surveillance in some of these cases. A similar number have been listed by military authorities as potentially chargeable in front of the military commissions established by the President—and now given congressional approval in the Military Commissions Act—but only ten have been actually charged as of this writing. After subtracting these three groups—those who have actually been released, those the government seeks to release, and those who still stand to be charged—we're left with a remainder on the order of 250 prisoners at Guantánamo who, it appears, after five years of severe confinement there, are deemed by their captors to be eligible for neither release nor charging. The plain inference is that their interrogators have come up with no evidence that they've been implicated in acts of terrorism but still consider them too dangerous to let go. These then—along with however many long-term prisoners might be locked away without charge in Iraq, Afghanistan, or other places where the United States continues to have some say over their fates—are the indefinitely detained of the war on terror.

If the "customary law of war" permits their continued imprisonment until the end of hostilities, their prospects seem exceedingly dim. Two questions bear on the legitimacy of their confinement: whether they have been rightly estimated to be part of a hostile enemy force or network and how it can be ascertained when hostilities have ended in this largely clandestine conflict. "Global War on Terror" may have had a certain ring as a battle cry, or at least some utility from a marketing standpoint as a brand name, but it muddies the detention issue, for it seems to imply that the US must remain at war, transforming itself into a permanent national security state, until terrorism—not any particular organized force but a diffuse phenomenon that has existed for more than a century—has been thoroughly banished from the world. In fact, Congress did not authorize a war on "terror" but granted the President authority

to use all necessary and appropriate force against those nations, organizations, or persons he determines planned, authorized, committed, or aided the terrorist attacks that occurred on September 11, 2001, or harbored such organizations or persons, in order to prevent any future acts of international terrorism against the United States by such nations, organizations or persons.

The administration sometimes acknowledges as much. "When administration officials refer to the war on terror," John Bellinger, the State Department's legal adviser, recently said, "we are not stating that we are in a legal state of armed conflict with every terrorist organization, everywhere in the world, at all times.... We do think we are in a legal state of armed conflict with al-Qaeda."

Subsumed under that definition, one assumes, are the Taliban in Afghanistan and the foreign fighters connected to the force known as al-Qaeda in Iraq. An end to fighting in Afghanistan and Iraq may be nowhere in sight, but at least when it does finally occur we'll presumably be able to recognize the fact. But how will anyone ever know whether the war with al-Qaeda has ended? An armistice cannot easily be imagined. Will the tribal regions along the border of Pakistan, where Osama bin Laden is supposed to be finding refuge, have to have been pacified? What methods could security officials use to certify that there is no network of "sleeper cells" remaining in the West? And if hopeful answers to these questions cannot easily be imagined, is it possible to imagine any political figure in authority declaring in the foreseeable future that this "war" has ended, or been sufficiently contained, to permit the release of supposed "hard-core" terrorist detainees at Guantánamo and elsewhere? If we look at the situation this way, the indefinite detention of combatants in this war seems not just open-ended but truly without limits, a predicament to which the "customary laws of war" do not offer an obvious answer.

The issue was much on the minds of some Supreme Court justices when oral arguments were heard nearly three years ago in the suit brought on behalf of Yaser Esam Hamdi, an American citizen by birth who'd been detained as "an illegal enemy combatant." Repeatedly Justices O'Connor, Souter, and Breyer pressed the government's lawyer to say when it might be appropriate for the courts to hear habeas petitions on behalf of prisoners held for many years in an unending conflict. "Doesn't the Court have some business intervening at some point, if it's the Hundred Years' War or something?" an impatient Stephen Breyer demanded. "We recognize the viability of the writ of habeas corpus," Paul D. Clement replied on the government's behalf. "There certainly is a challenge that can be brought to the length of the detention at some point."[4] When that point would come and how it would be recognized were questions left unanswered by the government. Those questions were obviously still on Justice O'Connor's mind when she wrote the opinion for the Court, holding that an American citizen designated as an "enemy combatant" was still entitled to due process and could not be imprisoned indefinitely without charge.

The plaintiff, she said, faced "the substantial prospect of perpetual detention." If one accepted the government's reasoning, she went on, "Hamdi's detention could last for the rest of his life." The ruling in *Hamdi* v. *Rumsfeld* established a legal double standard: indefinite detention without charge was now unacceptable for citizens but possibly quite all right for foreigners held in remote places by US armed forces and security agencies, though these foreign prisoners also faced "the substantial prospect of perpetual detention." At best, it could be said that, with *Hamdi* as a possible precedent, there was room for eventual judicial review on that point—until the passage of the Military

---

4. In his oral argument in the case of *Hamdan* v. *Rumsfeld* the following year, Clement suggested that the Authorization to Use Military Force resolution passed by Congress might imply the power to suspend habeas corpus in particular cases, given the so-called suspension clause in the Constitution, which says Congress can suspend the writ in instances of "invasion" and "insurrection." A suspension of the writ could be "constitutionally valid," he said, even if Congress "sort of stumbles on it" without the formal act envisioned in the Constitution. "You are leaving us," Justice Souter retorted, "with the position of the United States that the Congress may validly suspend [the writ] inadvertently."

Commissions Act in the fall of 2006, that is, which barred access to federal courts on habeas petitions by foreigners who had been designated as "illegal alien combatants." Now, even if a Democratic-led Congress succeeds in removing that bar—a big if for the next two years, given the possibility of a presidential veto—it could be two or three years before a test case reaches the highest court. By then the longest-serving Guantánamo prisoners would be into their eighth year of detention without charge, with no end in sight.

Inevitably, if the fate of "illegal enemy combatants" once again becomes an issue before the Supreme Court, the relevance of the Geneva Conventions will be debated as it was in June 2006 in the case of *Hamdan v. Rumsfeld*. The majority then held that one of the flaws in the presidential order establishing military commissions was their failure to conform to what's known as Common Article 3 of the conventions; specifically the failure of procedures that had been outlined to meet the article's broad and elevated requirement that they offer "all the judicial guarantees which are recognized as indispensable by civilized peoples." Writing for the Court, Justice John Paul Stevens noted that in the administration's tribunals, the accused could be denied access to the evidence against them. "Absent express statutory provision to the contrary," he said, "information used to convict a person of a crime must be disclosed to him."

The Military Commissions Act, drafted a few months later, was a direct response and challenge to the Stevens ruling. It provided statutory authority for withholding evidence from the accused "to protect from disclosure the sources, methods, or activities by which the United States acquired evidence." The Bush administration, of course, had argued from the start that the Geneva Conventions had no application to the struggle against a transnational terrorist group such as al-Qaeda. It now had to backtrack on its claim that the Constitution gave the president "plenary powers over military operations (including the treatment of prisoners)," but it retreated only slightly: while recognizing the existence of the Geneva Conventions, the same Military Commissions Act granted the president "authority for the United States to interpret the meaning and application of the Geneva conventions."[5] (In apparent contradiction, Congress claimed authority for itself to interpret the meaning of the Geneva treaties, flatly declaring that the tribunals it was authorizing met the requirements of Common Article 3, Justice Stevens notwithstanding.)

Here again it's open to question whether Democrats seeking to preserve something more than a marginal role for the judiciary on these issues will be able to get the votes needed to overturn a presidential veto, at least during the current Congress. Even if Democrats in the new Congress are blocked in their attempt to amend the Military Commissions Act, it could still make its way to the Supreme Court for review. Or a new administration and Congress, after 2008, could revisit some of these issues. What seems clear is that the question of indefinite detention won't simply disappear and will eventually need to be addressed.

Who then gets to interpret the Geneva Conventions could matter a great deal to supposedly "hard-core" prisoners held in indefinite detention without charge and with little or no prospect of release. Such detention is permitted by the conventions for enemy combatants granted prisoner-of-war status in an "international armed conflict."

---

5. The argument about the president's "plenary power" in matters involving prisoners was first made in a memo by John Yoo in January 2002 when he was head of the Office of Legal Counsel in the Justice Department. The administration has never quite given up on the claim. When it reached agreement with Republican holdouts in the Senate on the Military Commissions Act, it made a point of saying that President Bush had not needed congressional approval on issues involving interrogation standards that the act purported to address. "The President, of course, had authority to do this under his powers as Commander-in-Chief," Stephen J. Hadley, the national security adviser, said at a press briefing, "but what we wanted to do was to have an additional legal framework supported by the Congress." To have acknowledged that congressional authority had been necessary all along would have amounted to conceding that the President had been overstepping constitutional checks and balances for four years.

But there is no provision for indefinite detention in the cases of "protected persons" who have been detained but not charged in conflicts that don't meet that standard. Oblivious of contradiction, the administration has paid lip service to the Geneva standards—President Bush has repeatedly pledged to adhere to their "spirit"—while simultaneously implying that taking them literally could be at least inconvenient, possibly dangerous.

Strictly speaking, the government contended, the struggle against al-Qaeda couldn't be an "international armed conflict" because al-Qaeda isn't a state, or a "noninternational armed conflict" because it sprawls across the borders of many states. Therefore, government lawyers argued (until they lost the argument in the *Hamdan* case), there is a lacuna in the conventions. The administration, which places a low value on what's called international humanitarian law, came forward with no proposals on how to fill the lacuna it perceived. Instead, claiming a license to set its own standards unilaterally, it charged right through it. It's as if its legal advisers sought to apply to international law their usual conservative precepts about "strict construction" and "the intentions of the framers."

The fact that al-Qaeda wasn't foreseen when the conventions were agreed on in 1949, however, hardly negates a larger truth about the conventions, which the Supreme Court has now recognized: that they were intended in the judgment of most experts to be entirely comprehensive, setting minimal standards of humane treatment for illegal as well as legal combatants. No class of warrior was exempted from the minimal legal protections built into Common Article 3. These include a prohibition on "outrages upon personal dignity, in particular humiliating and degrading treatment" as well as "cruel treatment and torture." By now it's more than obvious this was the language that worried administration officials, intent as they were on sending a message to interrogators on the urgent need for "actionable intelligence" on terrorist networks.

It's possible to imagine a different kind of administration in which government lawyers might have worried about a different kind of lacuna in international law: the absence of any clear provision for preventive detention of fighters who view themselves as adherents of networks that spawn terrorist plots (and who therefore might reasonably be considered to be more dangerous than the traditional prisoner taken captive on a battlefield). With a view to maintaining alliances and building international support, such an administration might have thought about seeking an indictment of Osama bin Laden and his most conspicuous aides from the new International Criminal Court, which the United States has strenuously opposed under President Bush. It might have proposed negotiations on a new Geneva convention to cover the new situation. It might even have come forward to propose standards of due process for assessing and reassessing the threat posed by individual detainees. Dream on: that is clearly not the administration we are going to have for the next two years. It remains to be seen whether the new leadership at the Pentagon, following Donald Rumsfeld's departure, will be willing to address a question that clearly never weighed on him: the question—it's political as well as legal—of how long the system of indefinite detention can be sustained.

Tim Golden, in *The New York Times*, recently described a short-lived attempt by the military authorities at Guantánamo to make conditions there less severe. The plan even involved a new cellblock designed with an eye to encouraging communal exercise and meals, in conditions approaching those afforded traditional prisoners of war.[6] By the time the cellblock opened in December 2006, however, the military authorities had lost faith in the experiment. Following a riot and a mass suicide attempt in 2005 and three successful suicides in June 2006, they clamped down and restored the ban on group activities for the detainees. "I don't think there is such a thing as a

---

6. "Military Takes a Tougher Line with Detainees," *The New York Times*, December 10, 2006.

medium-security terrorist," Rear Admiral Harry B. Harris Jr. told the *Times* reporter. In other words, the authorities at Guantánamo are once again operating on the premise that Donald Rumsfeld first articulated five years ago—that the prisoners there are "the worst of the worst."

After the three prisoners successfully hung themselves from the wire-mesh framework of their cages in June, the commander of the detention center asserted that it was "not an act of desperation but an act of asymmetric warfare committed against us." That's a very convenient way of thinking. Another, less convenient, would be to grasp the possibility that desperation and a political outlook capable of inspiring "an act of asymmetric warfare" need not be mutually exclusive states of mind. Scores of unsuccessful suicide attempts at Guantánamo and mass hunger strikes, not to mention ordinary common sense, argue that more than a few of the prisoners have reached a state of desperation after more than five years of confinement that, for most of them, has included rounds of relentless interrogation, some of it, as we now know, grossly coercive, including isolation, sensory deprivation, stress positions, loud music, sexual taunting, and mockery of Islam. Instead of congratulating ourselves on allowing the prisoners to have Korans and listen to the call to prayers five times a day, we might renew the effort to ease the conditions of their day-to-day lives, which are harsher by some measures than conditions on death row in mainland prisons.

Even if we assume, for the purpose of discussion, that the military authorities are right in considering the indefinitely detained to be committed jihadists to a man, finding ways to ease the circumstances of their confinement might be seen as an investment in the possibility—however remote it may now seem—that they will one day return to their homelands. To put it another way, the government might take seriously the possibility that the US may one day be relieved of the political and moral burden involved in their perpetual detention without charge.

None of those released from Guantánamo has received an acknowledgment that there appear to have been no reasonable grounds for his detention, let alone an apology for the years snatched from his life, let alone even a modest attempt at compensation. In fact, Congress has had the foresight to bar damage suits by former detainees. Whenever questions are raised about cases in which reasonable grounds for suspicion are hardest to detect—the teenagers, septuagenarians, and Muslim travelers in war-afflicted regions who, whatever their motives or sentiments, never had a chance to get training as soldiers or bombers—official spokesmen can be relied on to allude to damning material in classified files that cannot be disclosed without damage to national security.

In some well-known cases such claims appear to be a matter of pure convenience—cases like that of Murat Kurnaz, a Turkish citizen, though born and raised in Germany. A couple of months after September 11, Kurnaz was pulled off a public bus in Pakistan at the age of nineteen and turned over to the Americans, who held him at Guantánamo until August 2006 when he was finally released at twenty-four. That was a year and a half after a federal judge, sitting on a habeas petition in his case, declared in open court that most of the evidence in his classified file was actually exculpatory and there was nothing to support suspicions of American interrogators that he had al-Qaeda ties. The purported "intelligence" said he'd been close to a successful suicide bomber named Selcuk Bilgin and that, since he hailed from Germany, he might also have been an associate of Mohamed Atta. The Bilgin Kurnaz knew turned out to be alive in Bremen and the connection to Atta had never been based on anything more than the fact that they were two devout Muslim males, among tens of thousands, who resided in Germany. The September 11 ringleader was an Arab from Cairo who'd lived in Hamburg; Kurnaz, a Turk from Bremen, seventy miles away, spoke no Arabic before arriving at Guantánamo. But how was he to prove that they'd never been acquainted? No one in authority was in any hurry, it seems, to clear up a case that revealed nothing except the inability of some American intelligence officers to look on a religious Muslim of fighting age and imagine that he might not be an enemy.[7]

Kurnaz, now home in Bremen, appears to have emerged from the Guantánamo cages psychologically and spiritually intact. There's the even more dismaying case of Jumah al-Dossari, a Saudi with Bahraini citizenship, who has attempted suicide twelve times, according to the official military count, and who's still being held at Guantánamo. The purpose of Guantánamo is to destroy people and he'd been destroyed, he told his New York lawyer, a young volunteer from the firm of Dorsey and Whitney named Joshua Colangelo-Bryan. He could no longer trust people, the prisoner said, and he had no hope. In his fifth year of detention without charge, with no release in sight, that did not sound like an irrational assessment of his circumstances.[8]

### POSTSCRIPT

This article appeared in *The New York Review of Books* of February 15, 2007. The US Supreme Court heard arguments at the end of 2007 on whether Congress had the power to suspend habeas corpus for prisoners held outside the United States, as it had done under the Military Commissions Act of 2006; and whether it had the power as well to limit the authority of federal courts in cases arising at Guantánamo. A ruling was expected by the end of the Court's term in June 2008. It was not expected to touch directly on the issue of indefinite detention without charge. By the time of the ruling most of the prisoners at Guantánamo will have been held for more than six years as "illegal enemy combatants."

—December 11, 2007

---

7. A dispatch on the Kurnaz case by Richard Bernstein appeared in *The New York Times* on June 5, 2005.

8. The al-Dossari case was described in detail by Stacy Sullivan in *New York* magazine, June 26, 2006.

# 3

# 'THE MOMENT HAS COME TO GET RID OF SADDAM'

## Mark Danner

*The only thing that worries me about you is your optimism.*

—Spanish Prime Minister José María Aznar
to President Bush,
February 22, 2003

SURELY ONE OF the agonizing attributes of our post–September 11 age is the unending need to reaffirm realities that have been proved, and proved again, but just as doggedly denied by those in power, forcing us to live trapped between two narratives of present history, the one gaining life and color and vigor as more facts become known, the other growing ever paler, brittler, more desiccated, but still sustained by the life support of official power.

At the center of our national life stands the master narrative of this bifurcated politics: the Iraq war, fought to eliminate the threat of weapons of mass destruction that turned out not to exist, brought to a quick and glorious conclusion on a sunlit aircraft carrier deck whose victory celebration almost instantly became a national embarrassment. That was four and a half years ago; the war's ending and indeed its beginning, so clearly defined for that single trembling instant, have long since vanished into contested history.

The latest entry in that history appeared on September 26, 2007, when the Spanish daily *El País* published a transcript of a discussion held on February 22, 2003—nearly a month before the war began—between President Bush and José María Aznar, then prime minister of Spain. (See the transcript on pages 52–58.) Though the leaders met at Mr. Bush's ranch in Crawford, Texas, some quickly dubbed the transcript Downing Street Memo II, and indeed the document does share some themes with that critical British memorandum, mostly in its clear demonstration of the gap between what President Bush and members of his administration were saying publicly during the run-up to the war and what they were saying, and doing, in more private settings. Though Hans Blix, the UN chief inspector whose teams were then scouring Iraq for the elusive weapons, had yet to deliver his report—two weeks later he would tell the Security Council that it would take not "years, nor weeks, but months" to complete "the key remaining disarmament tasks"—at Crawford the President shows himself impatient, even anxious, for war. "This is like Chinese water torture," he says of the inspections. "We have to put an end to it."

Even in discussing Aznar's main concern, the vital need to give the war international legitimacy by securing a second UN resolution justifying the use of force—a resolution that, catastrophically, was never achieved—little pretense is made that an invasion of Iraq is not already a certainty. "If anyone vetoes," the President tells Aznar,

> we'll go. Saddam Hussein isn't disarming. We have to catch him right now. Until now we've shown an incredible amount of patience. There are two weeks left. In two weeks we'll be militarily ready.... We'll be in Baghdad by the end of March.

The calendar has already been determined—not by the inspectors and what they might or might not find, nor by the diplomats and what they might or might not negotiate, but by the placement and readiness of warplanes and soldiers and tanks.

When did war become a certainty? The gradations of the President's attitudes are impossible to chart, though as far back as the previous July, the head of British intelligence, Sir Richard Dearlove, on his famous consultations in Washington, had detected "a perceptible shift in attitude." As Dearlove was quoted reporting to the British cabinet in the most famous passage in the Downing Street Memo:

> Military action was now seen as inevitable. Bush wanted to remove Saddam, through military action, justified by the conjunction of terrorism and WMD. But the intelligence and facts were being fixed around the policy. The NSC had no patience with the UN route. . . .[1]

It is on this point—the need of the Europeans to have a UN resolution justifying force, and thus a legal, or at least internationally legitimate, war, and the deep ambivalence among Bush administration officials about taking "the UN route"—that much of the drama of the Crawford transcript turns, making it into a kind of playlet pitting the sinuous, subtle, and sophisticated European, worried about the great opposition in Europe, and in Spain in particular, to an American-led war of choice with Iraq ("We need your help with our public opinion," Aznar tells Bush), against the blustery, impatient, firing-straight-from-the-hip American cowboy. Bush wants to put out the second resolution on Monday. Aznar says, "We'd prefer to wait

---

1. Dearlove's consultations had taken place in Washington and at CIA headquarters in Langley, Virginia, on July 20, 2002, and he reported to a meeting of the British "war cabinet" at Ten Downing Street three days later. See Mark Danner, *The Secret Way to War: The Downing Street Memo and the Iraq War's Buried History* (New York Review Books, 2006), pp. 6–7 and pp. 88–89.

until Tuesday." Bush counters, "Monday afternoon, taking the time zone differences into account." To Bush's complaint that the UN process was like "Chinese water torture," Aznar offers soothing understanding and a plea to take a breath:

> *Aznar*: I agree, but it would be good to be able to count on as many people as possible. Have a little patience.
> *Bush*: My patience has run out. I won't go beyond mid-March.
> *Aznar*: I'm not asking you to have indefinite patience. Simply that you do everything possible so that everything comes together.

Aznar, a right-wing Catholic idealist who believes in the human rights arguments for removing Saddam Hussein, finds himself on a political knife edge: more than nine Spaniards in ten oppose going to war and millions have just marched through the streets of Madrid in angry opposition; he is intensely concerned to gain a UN resolution making the war an internationally sanctioned effort and not just an American-led "aggression." Bush responds to his plea for diplomacy with a remarkable litany of threats directed at the current temporary members of the Security Council. "Countries like Mexico, Chile, Angola, and Cameroon have to know," the President declares, "that what's at stake is the United States' security and acting with a sense of friendship toward us." In case Aznar doesn't get the point, he describes to the Spaniard what each nation will suffer if it doesn't recognize "what's at stake":

> [Chilean President Ricardo] Lagos has to know that the Free Trade Agreement with Chile is pending Senate confirmation, and that a negative attitude on this issue could jeopardize that ratification. Angola is receiving funds from the Millennium Account that could also be compromised if they don't show a positive attitude. And Putin must know that his attitude is jeopardizing the relations of Russia and the United States.

What is striking about this passage is not only how crude and clumsy it is, with the President of the United States spouting threats like a movie gangster—he presumably wants the Spaniard to convey them directly to the various leaders—but how ineffective the bluster turned out to be. None of these countries changed their position on a second resolution, which, in the event, was never brought before the Security Council to what would have been certain defeat. Bush, in making the threats, did the one thing an effective leader is supposed always to avoid: he issued an order that was not obeyed, thus demonstrating the limits of his power. (The Iraq war itself, meant as it was to "shock and awe" the world and particularly US adversaries, did much the same thing.)

Along with bluster comes stern self-righteousness. Aznar asks whether "there's a possibility of Saddam Hussein going into exile"— "the biggest success," he tells the President, "would be to win the game without firing a single shot"—and Bush answers that there is. According to the Egyptians, Bush tells Aznar, Saddam has

> indicated that he's willing to go into exile if they let him take $1 billion and all the information that he wants about the weapons of mass destruction.

And would such exile, asks Aznar, come with a "guarantee" (presumably against prosecution or extradition)? "No guarantee," declares Bush. "He's a thief, a terrorist, a war criminal. Compared to Saddam, Milošević would be a Mother Teresa." Though it's hard to evaluate whether Saddam was really willing to leave Iraq—the Egyptians, Saudis, and others who were then touting the possibility all had an interest in seeing Saddam leave and the Sunni power structure remain in place—it is inconceivable that he would do so without some sort of guarantee, a possibility Bush forecloses.

What is most interesting in this passage, and indeed in the entire transcript, is what it reveals about Bush's attitudes and character. One moment he blusters and threatens, the next he speaks with reverence and self-righteousness about how he is guided by his "historic sense of responsibility":

> When some years from now History judges us, I don't want people to ask themselves why Bush, or Aznar, or Blair didn't face their responsibilities. In the end, what people want is to enjoy freedom. Not long ago, in Romania, I was reminded of the example of Ceauşescu: it took just one woman to call him a liar for the whole repressive system to come down. That's the unstoppable power of freedom. I am convinced that I'll get that resolution.

He did not get it, of course. Despite his strong conviction, neither Chile nor Angola nor Russia proved ready to change their votes, threat or no threat. Bush's conviction, here as elsewhere, came not from an independent analysis of the facts—of the interests and intentions of the nations involved—but from the wellspring of faith. He has confused rhetoric, however uplifting, and reality. Aznar, the sophisticated European, comments wryly on this. It is the most Jamesian moment in the playlet of Crawford; one can almost see the subtly arched eyebrow:

> *Aznar*: The only thing that worries me about you is your optimism.
> *Bush*: I am an optimist, because I believe that I'm right. I'm at peace with myself. It's up to us to face a serious threat to peace.

It is worrying, as Aznar remarks, to rely on optimism grounded only in belief. The Spaniard knows that gaining that second Security Council resolution, and thus the critical international legitimacy for the war, will be very hard; in many nations, launching a war against Iraq, particularly before the UN inspectors have finished their work, is deeply unpopular. Faith cannot replace facts, nor can a historic sense of mission. Both may be personally comforting—they plainly are to George W. Bush—but they don't obviate the need to know things.

Bush came to office a man who knew little of the world, who had hardly traveled outside the country, who knew nothing of the practice of foreign policy and diplomacy. Two years later, after the attacks of September 11 and his emergence as a self-described "war president," he has come to know only that this lack of knowledge is not a handicap but perhaps even a strength: that he doesn't need to know things in order to believe that he's right and to be at peace with himself. He has redefined his weakness—his lack of knowledge and experience—as his singular strength. He believes he's right. It is a matter of generations and destiny and freedom: it is "up to us to face a serious threat to peace." For Bush, faith, conviction, and a felt sense of destiny—not facts or knowledge—are the real necessities of leadership.[2]

2. And not just for George Bush. The mystique of leadership—of faith over facts—pulled others along in its wake. Condoleezza Rice, for example, makes a curious appearance in the discussion, assuring the President and the Spanish prime minister that she has "the impression" that Hans Blix, whose report is due the following week, "will now be more negative than before about the Iraqis' intentions." In fact, quite the opposite: Blix will tell the Security Council that "the key remaining disarmament tasks" can be achieved not in "years, nor weeks, but months." Here is what Blix told the Security Council on March 7, 2003:

> How much time would it take to resolve the key remaining disarmament tasks? While cooperation can and is to be immediate, disarmament and at any rate the verification of it cannot be instant. Even with a proactive Iraqi attitude, induced by continued outside pressure, it would still take some time to verify sites and items, analyse documents, interview relevant persons, and draw conclusions. It would not take years, nor weeks, but months. Neither governments nor inspectors would want disarmament inspection to go on forever. However, it must be remembered that in accordance with the governing resolutions, a sustained inspection and monitoring system is to remain in place after verified disarmament to give confidence and to strike an alarm, if signs were seen of the revival of any proscribed weapons programmes.

Blix's conclusions were not only *not* "more negative than before about the Iraqis' intentions," he suggests that inspections of all the suspect sites could be completed in a matter of months. President Bush, needless to say, is not willing to wait months, or even weeks,

So Bush is confident—confident about winning the second resolution and thus international legitimacy; confident, because "we're developing a very strong humanitarian aid package," that "there's a good basis for a better future" in a "post-Saddam Iraq." But there is a difference between being sure and being right. In fact, at the very moment he is telling these things to the Spanish prime minister in Crawford, Texas, the postwar planning in Washington is a shambles, consisting of little more than confusion and savage internecine warfare between the Defense and State departments.

The plan for governance in "post-Saddam Iraq" does not exist, all discussion of it having been paralyzed by a bitter dispute between officials in the Pentagon, State Department, and CIA that the President will never resolve. The Iraqi "civil society" that he tells Aznar is "relatively strong" will soon be decimated by the prolonged looting and chaos that follows on the entry of American troops into Baghdad. The "good bureaucracy" he boasts about in Iraq will shortly be destroyed by a radical de-Baathification ordered by the American proconsul that he almost certainly never approved. The Iraqi army that he decides in early March will be retained and used for reconstruction will instead be peremptorily dissolved, to catastrophic effect.

If these radical departures from the President's chosen plan have dampened his optimism and faith—or indeed have even led him to try to discover what happened—there is no evidence of it. When Bush's latest biographer, Robert Draper, asked him why the Iraqi army had not been kept intact, as the President had decided it should

---

for the additional inspections to be completed. What would have happened if he had been? On the one hand, the administration's willingness to delay might have secured a deal whereby additional countries would have supported "all means necessary" to deal with Saddam. On the other, the inspectors, given more time, would have discovered no weapons, likely leading the administration to argue that the inspections themselves were useless—not that the weapons didn't exist. But the momentum for war would have been blunted.

be, Bush replied, "Yeah, I can't remember. I'm sure I said, 'This is the policy, what happened?'"[3]

"This is the policy, what happened?" As a subtitle for a history of the Iraq war, one could certainly do worse. Prime Minister Aznar is gone now, having been fatally weakened by his support for the Iraq war and the failure to obtain United Nations support for it; almost exactly a year after the war began, jihadists targeted the Madrid train station, killing nearly two hundred Spaniards and sending the prime minister to electoral defeat. Tony Blair, the star of the Downing Street Memo, is gone as well, his popularity having never recovered from his staunch support of the war. President Bush, on the other hand, remains confident of victory, just as he was confident he would win that second UN resolution. There is little sign that his confidence is any more firmly rooted in reality now than it was then. Instead of reality we have faith—in himself, in the deity, in "the unstoppable power of human freedom." He stands as lead actor in his own narrative of history, a story that grows steadily paler and more contested, animated solely by the authority of official power. Nearly five years after launching the war that would fulfill his "historic sense of responsibility," George W. Bush remains "at peace with himself."

—October 11, 2007

---

3. According to the *New York Times* account of this exchange:

> Mr. Bush acknowledged one major failing of the early occupation of Iraq when he said of disbanding the Saddam Hussein–era military, "The policy was to keep the army intact; didn't happen."
>
> But when Mr. Draper pointed out that Mr. Bush's former Iraq administrator, L. Paul Bremer III, had gone ahead and forced the army's dissolution and then asked Mr. Bush how he reacted to that, Mr. Bush said, "Yeah, I can't remember, I'm sure I said, 'This is the policy, what happened?'" But, he added, "Again, Hadley's got notes on all of this stuff," referring to Stephen J. Hadley, his national security adviser.

See Jim Rutenberg, "In Book, Bush Peeks Ahead to His Legacy," *The New York Times*, September 2, 2007, and Robert Draper, *Dead Certain: The Presidency of George W. Bush* (Free Press, 2007), p. 211.

## THE CRAWFORD TRANSCRIPT

*Following is the transcript of the conversation between George W. Bush and José María Aznar in Crawford, Texas, on February 22, 2003. It was adapted, with the assistance of Scott Staton, from Álvaro Degives-Más's translation of a Spanish text originally published in* El País *on September 26, 2007.*

*President Bush*: We're in favor of obtaining a second resolution in the Security Council and we'd like to do it quickly. We'd like to announce it on Monday or Tuesday [February 24 or 25, 2003].

*Prime Minister Aznar*: Better on Tuesday, after the meeting of the European Union's General Affairs Council. It's important to maintain the momentum achieved by the resolution of the European Union summit [in Brussels, on Monday, February 17]. We'd prefer to wait until Tuesday.

*PB*: It could be Monday afternoon, taking the time zone differences into account. In any case, next week. We're looking at a resolution drafted in such a way that it doesn't contain mandatory elements, doesn't mention the use of force, and states that Saddam Hussein has been incapable of fulfilling his obligations. That kind of resolution can be voted for by lots of people. It would be similar to the one passed during Kosovo [on June 10, 1999].

*PMA*: Would it be presented to the Security Council before and independently of a parallel declaration?

*Condoleezza Rice*: In fact there won't be a parallel declaration. We're thinking about a resolution that would be as simple as possible, without too many details on compliance that Saddam could use as [an excuse to stall via] phases and consequently fail to meet. We're talking with Blix [the UN chief inspector] and others on his team, to get ideas that can help introduce the resolution.

*PB*: Saddam Hussein won't change and he'll continue playing games. The time has come to get rid of him. That's it. As for me, I'll try from now on to use a rhetoric that's as subtle as can be while we're seeking approval of the resolution. If anyone vetoes [Russia, China, and France together with the US and the UK have veto power in the Security Council, being permanent members], we'll go. Saddam Hussein isn't disarming. We have to catch him right now. Until now we've shown an incredible amount of patience. There are two weeks left. In two weeks we'll be militarily ready. I think we'll get the second resolution. In the Security Council we have the three Africans [Cameroon, Angola, and Guinea], the Chileans, the Mexicans. I'll talk to all of them, also Putin, naturally. We'll be in Baghdad by the end of March. There's a 15 percent chance that at that point Saddam Hussein will be dead or will have fled. But those possibilities don't exist until we've shown our resolve. The Egyptians are talking to Saddam Hussein. It seems that he's indicated that he's willing to go into exile if they let him take $1 billion and all the information that he wants about the weapons of mass destruction. [Muammar] Gaddafi has told Berlusconi that Saddam Hussein wants to go. Mubarak tells us that in those circumstances there are many possibilities that he'll be assassinated.

We'd like to act with the mandate of the United Nations. If we act militarily, we'll do it with great precision and focus very closely on our objectives. We'll decimate the loyal troops and the regular army will know quickly what it's about. We've sent a very clear message to Saddam's generals: we'll treat them as war criminals. We know that they've accumulated a huge amount of dynamite to blow up the bridges and other infrastructure, and blow up the oil wells. We've planned to occupy those wells very quickly. The Saudis will also help us by putting as much oil as necessary on the market. We're developing a very strong humanitarian aid package. We can win without destruction. We're already putting into effect a post-Saddam Iraq, and I believe there's a good basis for a better future. Iraq has a good bureaucracy and a civil society that's relatively strong. It could be organized into a federation. Meanwhile, we're doing all we can to attend to the political needs of our friends and allies.

*PMA*: It's very important to [be able to] count on a resolution. It isn't the same to act with it as without it. It would be very convenient to count on a majority in the Security Council that would support that resolution. In fact, having a majority is more important than anyone casting a veto. We think the content of the resolution should state, among other things, that Saddam Hussein has lost his opportunity.

*PB*: Yes, of course. That would be better than to make a reference to "all means necessary" [he refers to the standard UN resolution that authorizes the use of "all means necessary"].

*PMA*: Saddam Hussein hasn't cooperated, he hasn't disarmed, we should make a summary of his breaches and send a more elaborate message. That would, for example, allow Mexico to make a move [he refers to changing its position, opposed to the second resolution, that Aznar heard personally from President Vicente Fox on Friday, February 21 during a travel stop he made in Mexico City].

*PB*: The resolution will be tailored to help you as best it can. I don't care much about the content.

*PMA*: We'll send you some texts.

*PB*: We don't have any text. Just one condition: that Saddam Hussein disarms. We can't allow Saddam Hussein to stall until summer. After all, he's had four months already in this last phase, and that's more than sufficient time to disarm.

*PMA*: That text would help us sponsor it and be its coauthors, and convince many people to sponsor it.

*PB*: Perfect.

*PMA*: Next Wednesday [February 26] I'll meet with Chirac. The resolution will have started to circulate by then.

*PB*: That seems good to me. Chirac knows the reality perfectly. His intelligence services have explained it to him. The Arabs are sending Chirac a very clear message: Saddam Hussein should go. The problem is that Chirac thinks he's Mister Arab, and in reality he's making life impossible for them. But I don't want any rivalry with Chirac. We have different points of view, but I would want that to be all. Give him my best regards. Really! The less he feels that rivalry exists between us, the better for all of us.

*PMA*: How will the resolution and the inspectors' report be combined?

*Condoleezza Rice*: Actually there won't be a report on February 28, the inspectors will present a written report on March 1, and their appearance before the Security Council won't happen until March 6 or 7 of 2003. We don't expect much from that report. As with the previous ones, it will be six of one and half a dozen of the other.

I have the impression that Blix will now be more negative than before about the Iraqis' intentions. After the inspectors have appeared before the Council we should anticipate the vote on the resolution taking place one week later. Meanwhile, the Iraqis will try to explain that they're meeting their obligations. It's neither true nor sufficient, even if they announce the destruction of some missiles.

*PB*: This is like Chinese water torture. We have to put an end to it.

*PMA*: I agree, but it would be good to be able to count on as many people as possible. Have a little patience.

*PB*: My patience has run out. I won't go beyond mid-March.

*PMA*: I'm not asking you to have indefinite patience. Simply that you do everything possible so that everything comes together.

*PB*: Countries like Mexico, Chile, Angola, and Cameroon have to know that what's at stake is the United States' security and acting with a sense of friendship toward us.

[Chilean President Ricardo] Lagos has to know that the Free Trade Agreement with Chile is pending Senate confirmation, and that a negative attitude on this issue could jeopardize that ratification. Angola is receiving funds from the Millennium Account that could also be compromised if they don't show a positive attitude. And Putin must know that his attitude is jeopardizing the relations of Russia and the United States.

*PMA*: Tony [Blair] would like to extend to the 14th.

*PB*: I prefer the 10th. This is like good cop, bad cop. I don't mind being the bad cop and that Blair be the good one.

*PMA*: Is it true that there's a possibility of Saddam Hussein going into exile?

*PB*: Yes, that possibility exists. Even that he gets assassinated.

*PMA*: An exile with some guarantee?

*PB*: No guarantee. He's a thief, a terrorist, a war criminal. Compared to Saddam, Milošević would be a Mother Teresa. When we go in, we'll uncover many more crimes and we'll take him to the International Court of Justice in The Hague. Saddam Hussein believes he's already gotten away. He thinks France and Germany have stopped holding him to his responsibilities. He also thinks that the protests of last week [Saturday, February 15] protect him. And he thinks I'm much weakened. But the people around him know that things are different. They know his future is in exile or in a coffin. That's why it's so important to keep the pressure on him. Gaddafi tells us indirectly that this is the only thing that can finish him. Saddam Hussein's sole strategy is to stall, stall, and stall.

*PMA*: In reality, the biggest success would be to win the game without firing a single shot while going into Baghdad.

*PB*: For me it would be the perfect solution. I don't want the war. I know what wars are like. I know the destruction and the death that comes with them. I am the one who has to comfort the mothers and the widows of the dead. Of course, for us that would be the best solution. Besides, it would save us $50 billion.

*PMA*: We need your help with our public opinion.

*PB*: We'll do everything we can. On Wednesday I'll talk about the situation in the Middle East, and propose a new peace framework that you know, and about the weapons of mass destruction, the benefits of a free society, and I'll place the history of Iraq in a wider context. Maybe that's of help to you.

*PMA*: What we are doing is a very profound change for Spain and the Spaniards. We're changing the politics that the country has followed over the last two hundred years.

*PB*: I am just as much guided by a historic sense of responsibility as you are. When some years from now History judges us, I don't want people to ask themselves why Bush, or Aznar, or Blair didn't face their responsibilities. In the end, what people want is to enjoy freedom. Not long ago, in Romania, I was reminded of the example of Ceauşescu: it took just one woman to call him a liar for the whole repressive system to come down. That's the unstoppable power of freedom. I am convinced that I'll get that resolution.

*PMA*: That would be the best.

*PB*: I made the decision to go to the Security Council. In spite of the disagreements within my administration, I told my people that we should work with our friends. It would be wonderful to have a second resolution.

*PMA*: The only thing that worries me about you is your optimism.

*PB*: I am an optimist, because I believe that I'm right. I'm at peace with myself. It's up to us to face a serious threat to peace. It annoys me to no end to contemplate the insensitivity of the Europeans toward the suffering Saddam Hussein inflicts on the Iraqis. Perhaps because he's dark, far away, and a Muslim, many Europeans think that everything is fine with him. I won't forget what [former NATO Secretary General, the Spaniard Javier] Solana once asked me: why we Americans think the Europeans are anti-Semites and incapable of facing their responsibilities. That defensive attitude is terrible. I have to admit that I have a splendid relationship with Kofi Annan.

*PMA*: He shares your ethical concerns.

*PB*: The more the Europeans attack me, the stronger I am in the United States.

*PMA*: We will have to make your strength compatible with the support of the Europeans.

# 4

## THE VICTOR?

### Peter Galbraith

IN HIS CONTINUING effort to bolster support for the Iraq war, President Bush traveled to Reno, Nevada, on August 28, 2007, to speak to the annual convention of the American Legion. He emphatically warned of the Iranian threat should the United States withdraw from Iraq. Said the President, "For all those who ask whether the fight in Iraq is worth it, imagine an Iraq where militia groups backed by Iran control large parts of the country."

On the same day, in the southern Iraqi city of Karbala, the Mahdi Army, a militia loyal to the radical Shiite cleric Moqtada al-Sadr, battled government security forces around the shrine of Imam Hussein, one of Shiite Islam's holiest places. A million pilgrims were in the city and fifty-one died.

The US did not directly intervene, but American jets flew overhead in support of the government security forces. As elsewhere in the south, those Iraqi forces are dominated by the Badr Organization, a militia founded, trained, armed, and financed by Iran. When US forces ousted Saddam's regime from the south in early April 2003, the Badr Organization infiltrated from Iran to fill the void left by the Bush administration's failure to plan for security and governance in post-invasion Iraq.

In the months that followed, the US-run Coalition Provisional Authority (CPA) appointed Badr Organization leaders to key positions in Iraq's American-created army and police. At the same time, L. Paul Bremer's CPA appointed party officials from the Supreme Council for Islamic Revolution in Iraq (SCIRI) to be governors and serve on governorate councils throughout southern Iraq. SCIRI, recently renamed the Supreme Islamic Iraqi Council (SIIC), was founded at the Ayatollah Khomeini's direction in Tehran in 1982. The Badr Organization is the militia associated with SCIRI.

In the January 2005 elections, SCIRI became the most important component of Iraq's ruling Shiite coalition. In exchange for not taking the prime minister's slot, SCIRI won the right to name key ministers, including the minister of the interior. From that ministry, SCIRI placed Badr militiamen throughout Iraq's national police.

In short, George W. Bush had from the first facilitated the very event he warned would be a disastrous consequence of a US withdrawal from Iraq: the takeover of a large part of the country by an Iranian-backed militia. And while the President contrasts the promise of democracy in Iraq with the tyranny in Iran, there is now substantially more personal freedom in Iran than in southern Iraq.

Iran's role in Iraq is pervasive, but also subtle. When Iraq drafted its permanent constitution in 2005, the American ambassador energetically engaged in all parts of the process. But behind the scenes, the Iranian ambassador intervened to block provisions that Tehran did not like. As it happened, both the Americans and the Iranians wanted to strengthen Iraq's central government. While the Bush administration clung to the mirage of a single Iraqi people, Tehran worked to give its proxies, the pro-Iranian Iraqis it supported—by then established as the government of Iraq—as much power as possible. (Thanks to Kurdish obstinacy, neither the US nor Iran succeeded in its goal, but even now both the US and Iran want to see the central government strengthened.)

Since 2005, Iraq's Shiite-led government has concluded numerous economic, political, and military agreements with Iran. The most

important would link the two countries' strategic oil reserves by building a pipeline from southern Iraq to Iran, while another commits Iran to providing extensive military assistance to the Iraqi government. According to a senior official in Iraq's Oil Ministry, smugglers divert at least 150,000 barrels of Iraq's daily oil exports through Iran, a figure that approaches 10 percent of Iraq's production. Iran has yet to provide the military support it promised to the Iraqi army. With the US supplying 160,000 troops and hundreds of billions of dollars to support a pro-Iranian Iraqi government, Iran has no reason to invest its own resources.

Of all the unintended consequences of the Iraq war, Iran's strategic victory is the most far-reaching. In establishing the border between the Ottoman Empire and the Persian Empire in 1639, the Treaty of Qasr-i-Shirin demarcated the boundary between Sunni-ruled lands and Shiite-ruled lands. For eight years of brutal warfare in the 1980s, Iran tried to breach that line but could not. (At the time, the Reagan administration supported Saddam Hussein precisely because it feared the strategic consequences of an Iraq dominated by Iran's allies.) The 2003 US invasion of Iraq accomplished what Khomeini's army could not. Today, the Shiite-controlled lands extend to the borders of Kuwait and Saudi Arabia. Bahrain, a Persian Gulf kingdom with a Shiite majority and a Sunni monarch, is most affected by these developments; but so is Saudi Arabia's Eastern Province, which is home to most of the kingdom's Shiites. (They may even be a majority in the province but this is unknown as Saudi Arabia has not dared to conduct a census.) The US Navy has its most important Persian Gulf base in Bahrain while most of Saudi Arabia's oil is under the Eastern Province.

America's Iraq quagmire has given new life to Iran's Syrian ally, Bashir Assad. In 2003, the Syrian Baathist regime seemed an anachronism unable to survive the region's political and economic changes. Today, Assad appears firmly in control, having even recovered from

the opprobrium of having his regime caught red-handed in the assassination of former Lebanese Prime Minister Rafik Hariri. In Lebanon, Hezbollah enjoys greatly enhanced stature for having held off the Israelis in the 2006 war. As Hezbollah's sponsor and source of arms, Iran now has an influence both in the Levant and in the Arab–Israeli conflict that it never before had.

The scale of the American miscalculation is striking. Before the Iraq war began, its neoconservative architects argued that conferring power on Iraq's Shiites would serve to undermine Iran because Iraq's Shiites, controlling the faith's two holiest cities, would, in the words of then Deputy Defense Secretary Paul Wolfowitz, be "an independent source of authority for the Shia religion emerging in a country that is democratic and pro-Western." Further, they argued, Iran could never dominate Iraq, because the Iraqi Shiites are Arabs and the Iranian Shiites Persian. It was a theory that, unfortunately, had no connection to reality.

Iran's bond with the Iraqi Shiites goes far beyond the support Iran gave Shiite leaders in their struggle with Saddam Hussein. Decades of oppression have made their religious identity more important to Iraqi Shiites than their Arab ethnic identity. (Also, many Iraqi Shiites have Turcoman, Persian, or Kurdish ancestors.) While Sunnis identify with the Arab world, Iraqi Shiites identify with the Shiite world, and for many this means Iran.

There is also the legacy of February 15, 1991, when President George H. W. Bush called on the Iraqi people to rise up against Saddam Hussein. Two weeks later, the Shiites in southern Iraq did just that. When Saddam's Republican Guards moved south to crush the rebellion, President Bush went fishing and no help was given. Only Iran showed sympathy. Hundreds of thousands died and no Iraqi Shiite I know thinks this failure of US support was anything but intentional. In assessing the loyalty of the Iraqi Shiites before the war, the war's architects often stressed how Iraqi Shiite conscripts fought

loyally for Iraq in the Iran–Iraq War. They never mentioned the 1991 betrayal. This was understandable: at the end of the 1991 war, Wolfowitz was the number-three man at the Pentagon, Dick Cheney was the defense secretary, and, of course, Bush's father was the president.

Iran and its Iraqi allies control, respectively, the Middle East's third- and second-largest oil reserves. Iran's influence now extends to the borders of the Saudi province that holds the world's largest oil reserves. President Bush has responded to these strategic changes wrought by his own policies by strongly supporting a pro-Iranian government in Baghdad and by arming and training the most pro-Iranian elements in the Iraqi military and police.

Beginning with his 2002 State of the Union speech, President Bush has articulated two main US goals for Iran: (1) the replacement of Iran's theocratic regime with a liberal democracy, and (2) preventing Iran from acquiring nuclear weapons. Since events in Iraq took a bad turn, he has added a third objective: gaining Iranian cooperation in Iraq.

The administration's track record is not impressive. The prospects for liberal democracy in Iran took a severe blow when reform-minded President Mohammad Khatami was replaced by the hard-line—and somewhat erratic—Mahmoud Ahmadinejad in August 2005. (Khatami had won two landslide elections which were a vote to soften the ruling theocracy; he was then prevented by the conservative clerics from accomplishing much.) At the time President Bush first proclaimed his intention to keep nuclear weapons out of Iranian hands, Iran had no means of making fissile material. Since then, however, Iran has defied the IAEA and the UN Security Council to assemble and use the centrifuges needed to enrich uranium. In Iraq, the administration accuses Iran of supplying particularly potent roadside bombs to Shiite militias and Sunni insurgents.

To coerce Iran into ceasing its uranium enrichment program, the Bush administration has relied on UN sanctions, the efforts of a

European negotiating team, and stern presidential warnings. The mismanaged Iraq war has undercut all these efforts. After seeing the US go to the United Nations with allegedly irrefutable evidence that Iraq possessed chemical and biological weapons and had a covert nuclear program, foreign governments and publics are understandably skeptical about the veracity of Bush administration statements on Iran. The Iraq experience makes many countries reluctant to support meaningful sanctions not only because they doubt administration statements but because they are afraid President Bush will interpret any Security Council resolution condemning Iran as an authorization for war.

With so much of the US military tied up in Iraq, the Iranians do not believe the US has the resources to attack them and then deal with the consequences. They know that a US attack on Iran would have little support in the US—it is doubtful that Congress would authorize it—and none internationally. Not even the British would go along with a military strike on Iran. President Bush's warnings count for little with Tehran because he now has a long record of tough language unmatched by action. As long as the Iranians believe the United States has no military option, they have limited incentives to reach an agreement, especially with the Europeans.

The administration's efforts to change Iran's regime have been feeble or feckless. President Bush's freedom rhetoric is supported by Radio Farda, a US-sponsored Persian language radio station, and a $75 million appropriation to finance Iranian opposition activities including satellite broadcasts by Los Angeles–based exiles. If only regime change was so easily accomplished!

The identity of Iranian recipients of US funding is secret but the administration's neoconservative allies have loudly promoted US military and financial support for Iranian opposition groups as diverse as the son of the late Shah, Iranian Kurdish separatists, and the Mujahideen-e-Khalq (MEK), which is on the State Department's list of terrorist organizations. Some of the Los Angeles exiles now being

funded are associated with the son of the Shah but it is unlikely that either the MEK or the Kurdish separatists would receive any of the $75 million. US secrecy—and that the administration treats the MEK differently from other terrorist organizations—has roused Iranian suspicions that the US is supporting these groups either through the democracy program or a separate covert action.

None of these groups is a plausible agent for regime change. The Shah's son represents a discredited monarchy and corrupt family. Iranian Kurdistan is seething with discontent, and Iranian security forces have suppressed large anti-regime demonstrations there. Kurdish nationalism on the margins of Iran, however, does not weaken the Iranian regime at the center. (While the US State Department has placed the PKK—a Kurdish rebel movement in Turkey—on its list of terrorist organizations, Pejak, the PKK's Iranian branch, is not on the list and its leaders even visit the US.)

The Mujahideen-e-Khalq is one of the oldest—and nastiest—of the Iranian opposition groups. After originally supporting the Iranian revolution, the MEK broke with Khomeini and relocated to Iraq in the early stages of the Iran–Iraq War. It was so closely connected to Saddam that MEK fighters not only assisted the Iraqis in the Iran–Iraq War but also helped Saddam put down the 1991 Kurdish uprising. While claiming to be democratic and pro-Western, the MEK closely resembles a cult. In April 2003, when I visited Camp Ashraf, its main base northeast of Baghdad, I found robotlike hero worship of the MEK leaders, Massoud and Maryam Rajavi; the fighters I met parroted a revolutionary party line, and there were transparently crude efforts at propaganda. To emphasize its being a modern organization as distinct from the Tehran theocrats, the MEK appointed a woman as Camp Ashraf's nominal commander and maintained a women's tank battalion. The commander was clearly not in command and the women mechanics supposedly working on tank engines all had spotless uniforms.

Both the US State Department and Iran view the MEK as a terrorist group. The US government, however, does not always act as if the MEK were one. During the 2003 invasion of Iraq, the US military dropped a single bomb on Camp Ashraf. It struck the women's barracks at a time of day when the soldiers were not there. When I visited two weeks later with an ABC camera crew, we filmed the MEK bringing a scavenged Iraqi tank into their base. US forces drove in and out of Camp Ashraf, making no effort to detain the supposed terrorists or to stop them from collecting Iraqi heavy weapons. Since Iran had its agents in Iraq from the time Saddam fell (and may have been doing its own scavenging of weapons), one can presume that this behavior did not go unnoticed. Subsequently, the US military did disarm the MEK, but in spite of hostility from both the Shiites and Kurds who now jointly dominate Iraq's government, its fighters are still at Camp Ashraf. Rightly or wrongly, many Iranians conclude from this that the US is supporting a terrorist organization that is fomenting violence inside Iran.

In fact, halting Iran's nuclear program and changing its regime are incompatible objectives. Iran is highly unlikely to agree to a negotiated solution with the US (or the Europeans) while the US is trying to overthrow its government. Air strikes may destroy Iran's nuclear facilities but they will rally popular support for the regime and give it a further pretext to crack down on the opposition.

From the perspective of US national security strategy, the choice should be easy. Iran's most prominent democrats have stated publicly that they do not want US support. In a recent open letter to be sent to UN Secretary General Ban Ki-moon, the Iranian dissident Akbar Ganji criticizes both the Iranian regime and US hypocrisy. "Far from helping the development of democracy," he writes, "US policy over the past 50 years has consistently been to the detriment of the proponents of freedom and democracy in Iran.... The Bush Administration, for its part, by approving a fund for democracy assistance in

Iran, which is in fact being largely spent on official institutions and media affiliated with the US government, has made it easy for the Iranian regime to describe its opponents as mercenaries of the US and to crush them with impunity."

Even though they can't accomplish it, the Bush administration leaders have been unwilling to abandon regime change as a goal. Its advocates compare their efforts to the support the US gave democrats behind the Iron Curtain over many decades. But there is a crucial difference. The Soviet and East European dissidents wanted US support, which was sometimes personally costly but politically welcome. But this is immaterial to administration ideologues. They are, to borrow Jeane Kirkpatrick's phrase, deeply committed to policies that feel good rather than do good. If Congress wants to help the Iranian opposition, it should cut off funding for Iranian democracy programs.

Right now, the US is in the worst possible position. It is identified with the most discredited part of the Iranian opposition and unwanted by the reformers who have the most appeal to Iranians. Many Iranians believe that the US is fomenting violence inside their country, and this becomes a pretext for attacks on US troops in Iraq. And for its pains, the US accomplishes nothing.

For eighteen years, Iran had a secret program aimed at acquiring the technology that could make nuclear weapons. A. Q. Khan, the supposedly rogue head of Pakistan's nuclear program, provided centrifuges to enrich uranium and bomb designs. When the Khan network was exposed, Iran declared in October 2003 its enrichment program to the International Atomic Energy Agency (IAEA), provided an accounting (perhaps not complete) of its nuclear activities, and agreed to suspend its uranium enrichment. Following the election of Ahmadinejad as president in 2005, Iran announced it would resume its uranium enrichment activities. During the last two years, it has assembled cascades of centrifuges and apparently enriched a small

amount of uranium to the 5 percent level required for certain types of nuclear power reactors (weapons require 80 to 90 percent enrichment but this is not technically very difficult once the initial enrichment processes are mastered).

The United States has two options for dealing with Iran's nuclear facilities: military strikes to destroy them or negotiations to neutralize them. The first is risky and the second may not produce results. So far, the Bush administration has not pursued either option, preferring UN sanctions (which, so far, have been more symbolic than punitive) and relying on Europeans to take the lead in negotiations. But neither sanctions nor the European initiative is likely to work. As long as Iran's primary concern is the United States, it is unlikely to settle for a deal that involves only Europe.

Sustained air strikes probably could halt Iran's nuclear program. While some Iranian facilities may be hidden and others protected deep underground, the locations of major facilities are known. Even if it is not possible to destroy all the facilities, Iran's scientists, engineers, and construction crews are unlikely to show up for work at places that are subject to ongoing bombing.

But the risks from air strikes are great. Many of the potential targets are in populated places, endangering civilians both from errant bombs and the possible dispersal of radioactive material. The rest of the world would condemn the attacks and there would likely be a virulent anti-US reaction in the Islamic world. In retaliation, Iran could wreak havoc on the world economy (and its own) by withholding oil from the global market and by military action to close the Persian Gulf shipping lanes.

The main risk to the US comes in Iraq. Faced with choosing between the US and Iran, Iraq's government may not choose its liberator. And even if the Iraqi government did not openly cooperate with the Iranians, pro-Iranian elements in the US-armed military and police almost certainly would facilitate attacks on US troops by

pro-Iranian Iraqi militia or by Iranian forces infiltrated across Iraq's porous border. A few days after Bush's August 28 speech, Iranian General Rahim Yahya Safavi underscored Iran's ability to retaliate, saying of US troops in the region: "We have accurately identified all their camps." Unless he chooses to act with reckless disregard for the safety of US troops in Iraq, President Bush has effectively denied himself a military option for dealing with the Iranian nuclear program.

A diplomatic solution to the crisis created by Iran's nuclear program is clearly preferable, but not necessarily achievable. Broadly speaking, states want nuclear weapons for two reasons: security and prestige. Under the Shah, Iran had a nuclear program but Khomeini disbanded it after the revolution on the grounds that nuclear weapons were un-Islamic. When the program resumed covertly in the mid-1980s, Iran's primary security concern was Iraq. At that time, Iraq had its own covert nuclear program; more immediately, it had threatened Iran with chemical weapons attacks on its cities. An Iranian nuclear weapon could serve as a deterrent to both Iraqi chemical and nuclear weapons.

With Iraq's defeat in the first Gulf War, the Iraqi threat greatly diminished. And of course it vanished after Iran's allies took power in Baghdad after the 2003 invasion. Today, Iran sees the United States as the main threat to its security. American military forces surround Iran—in Afghanistan, Iraq, Central Asia, and on the Persian Gulf. President Bush and his top aides repeatedly express solidarity with the Iranian people against their government while the US finances programs aimed at the government's ouster. The American and international press are full of speculation that Vice President Cheney wants Bush to attack Iran before his term ends. From an Iranian perspective, all this smoke could indicate a fire.

In 2003, as Trita Parsi's *Treacherous Alliance** shows, there was

---

*Treacherous Alliance: The Secret Dealings of Israel, Iran, and the United States* (Yale University Press, 2007).

PETER GALBRAITH

enough common ground for a deal. In May 2003, the Iranian authorities sent a proposal through the Swiss ambassador in Tehran, Tim
Guldimann, for negotiations on a package deal in which Iran would
freeze its nuclear program in exchange for an end to US hostility. The
Iranian paper offered "full transparency for security that there are no
Iranian endeavors to develop or possess WMD [and] full cooperation
with the IAEA based on Iranian adoption of all relevant instruments."
The Iranians also offered support for "the establishment of democratic institutions and a non-religious government" in Iraq; full cooperation against terrorists (including "above all, al-Qaeda"); and an
end to material support to Palestinian groups like Hamas. In return,
the Iranians asked that their country not be on the terrorism list or
designated part of the "axis of evil"; that all sanctions end; that the
US support Iran's claims for reparations for the Iran–Iraq War as part
of the overall settlement of the Iraqi debt; that they have access to
peaceful nuclear technology; and that the US pursue anti-Iranian terrorists, including "above all" the MEK. MEK members should, the Iranians said, be repatriated to Iran.

Basking in the glory of "Mission Accomplished" in Iraq, the Bush
administration dismissed the Iranian offer and criticized Guldimann
for even presenting it. Several years later, the Bush administration's
abrupt rejection of the Iranian offer began to look blatantly foolish
and the administration moved to suppress the story. Flynt Leverett,
who had handled Iran in 2003 for the National Security Council,
tried to write about it in *The New York Times* and found his Op-Ed
crudely censored by the NSC, which had to clear it. Guldimann, however, had given the Iranian paper to Ohio Republican Congressman
Bob Ney, now remembered both for renaming House cafeteria food
and for larceny. (As chairman of the House Administration Committee he renamed French fries "freedom fries" and is now in federal
prison for bribery.) I was surprised to learn that Ney had a serious
side. He had lived in Iran before the revolution, spoke Farsi, and

wanted better relations between the two countries. Trita Parsi, Ney's staffer in 2003, describes in detail the Iranian offer and the Bush administration's high-handed rejection of it in his wonderfully informative account of the triangular relationship among the US, Iran, and Israel, *Treacherous Alliance: The Secret Dealings of Israel, Iran, and the United States.*

Four years later, Iran holds a much stronger hand while the mismanagement of the Iraq occupation has made the US position incomparably weaker. While the 2003 proposal could not have been presented without support from the clerics who really run Iran, Iran's current president, Mahmoud Ahmadinejad, has made uranium enrichment the centerpiece of his administration and the embodiment of Iranian nationalism. Even though Ahmadinejad does not make decisions about Iran's nuclear program (and his finger would never be on the button if Iran had a bomb), he has made it politically very difficult for the clerics to come back to the 2003 paper.

Nonetheless, the 2003 Iranian paper could provide a starting point for a US–Iran deal. In recent years, various ideas have emerged that could accommodate both Iran's insistence on its right to nuclear technology and the international community's desire for iron-clad assurances that Iran will not divert the technology into weapons. These include a Russian proposal that Iran enrich uranium on Russian territory and also an idea floated by US and Iranian experts to have a European consortium conduct the enrichment in Iran under international supervision. Iran rejected the Russian proposal, but if hostility between Iran and the US were to be reduced, it might be revived. (The consortium idea has no official standing at this point.) While there are good reasons to doubt Iranian statements that its program is entirely peaceful, Iran remains a party to the Nuclear Non-Proliferation Treaty and its leaders, including Ahmadinejad, insist it has no intention of developing nuclear weapons. As long as this is the case, Iran could make a deal to limit its nuclear program without losing face.

From the inception of Iran's nuclear program under the Shah, prestige and the desire for recognition have been motivating factors. Iranians want the world, and especially the US, to see Iran as they do themselves—as a populous, powerful, and responsible country that is heir to a great empire and home to a 2,500-year-old civilization. In Iranian eyes, the US has behaved in a way that continually diminishes their country. Many Iranians still seethe over the US involvement in the 1953 coup that overthrew the government of democratically elected Prime Minister Mohammad Mossadegh and reinstated the Shah. Being designated a terrorist state and part of an "axis of evil" grates on the Iranians in the same way. In some ways, the 1979–1981 hostage crisis and Iran's nuclear program were different strategies to compel US respect for Iran. A diplomatic overture toward Iran might include ways to show respect for Iranian civilization (which is different from approval of its leaders) and could include an open apology for the US role in the 1953 coup, which, as it turned out, was a horrible mistake for US interests.

While President Bush insists that time is not on America's side, the process of negotiation—and even an interim agreement—might provide time for more moderate Iranians to assert themselves. So far as Iran's security is concerned, possession of nuclear weapons is more a liability than an asset. Iran's size—and the certainty of strong resistance —is sufficient deterrent to any US invasion, which, even at the height of the administration's post-Saddam euphoria, was never seriously considered. Developing nuclear weapons would provide Iran with no additional deterrent to a US invasion but could invite an attack.

Should al-Qaeda or another terrorist organization succeed in detonating a nuclear weapon in a US city, any US president will look to the country that supplied the weapon as a place to retaliate. If the origin of the bomb were unknown, a nuclear Iran—a designated state sponsor of terrorism—would find itself a likely target, even though it is extremely unlikely to supply such a weapon to al-Qaeda, a Sunni

fundamentalist organization. With its allies now largely running the government in Baghdad, Iran does not need a nuclear weapon to deter a hostile Iraq. An Iranian bomb, however, likely would cause Saudi Arabia to acquire nuclear weapons, thus canceling Iran's considerable manpower advantage over its Gulf rival. More pragmatic leaders, such as former President Akbar Hashemi Rafsanjani, may understand this. Rafsanjani, who lost the 2005 presidential elections to Ahmadinejad, is making a comeback, defeating a hard-liner to become chairman of Iran's Assembly of Experts for the Leadership (Majles-e Khobrgran Rahbari), which appoints and can dismiss the Supreme Leader.

At this stage, neither the US nor Iran seems willing to talk directly about bilateral issues apart from Iraq. Even if the two sides did talk, there is no guarantee that an agreement could be reached. And if an agreement were reached, it would certainly be short of what the US might want. But the test of a US–Iran negotiation is not how it measures up against an ideal arrangement but how it measures up against the alternatives of bombing or doing nothing.

US pre-war intelligence on Iraq was horrifically wrong on the key question of Iraq's possession of WMDs, and President Bush ignored the intelligence to assert falsely a connection between Saddam Hussein and September 11. This alone is sufficient reason to be skeptical of the Bush administration's statements on Iran.

On December 3, 2007, the US intelligence community undercut President Bush's case against Iran and shredded his already diminished credibility. As required by Congress, the National Intelligence Council published an unclassified version of its just-completed National Intelligence Estimate (NIE) on Iran's nuclear program. In its main conclusion, all sixteen US intelligence agencies declared: "We judge with high confidence that in fall 2003, Tehran halted its nuclear weapons program." This assessment eliminated any basis for a US attack on Iran, and even several leading neoconservatives unhappily

conceded in print that war was "off the table" and the US might have to consider negotiations to resolve issues relating to Iran's acquisition of nuclear technology.

On October 17, 2007—six weeks before the NIE was made public—President Bush had held a press conference at the White House. Russian President Vladimir Putin was in Iran on a state visit and had said he saw "no evidence to suggest Iran wants to build a nuclear bomb." Bush was asked about this:

Q. But you definitively believe Iran wants to build a nuclear weapon?

*The President*: I think so long—until they suspend and/or make it clear that they—that their statements aren't real, yeah, I believe they want to have the capacity, the knowledge, in order to make a nuclear weapon. And I know it's in the world's interest to prevent them from doing so. I believe that the Iranian—if Iran had a nuclear weapon, it would be a dangerous threat to world peace.

But this—we got a leader in Iran who has announced that he wants to destroy Israel. So I've told people that if you're interested in avoiding World War III, it seems like you ought to be interested in preventing them from having the knowledge necessary to make a nuclear weapon.

The CIA had already briefed Bush on the substance of the NIE, without any apparent effect. The episode provided another example of the irrelevance of strategy to President Bush's conduct of national security policy. Even if he believed, in his now famous gut, that the NIE's conclusions were wrong, he could only damage his goal of building international and domestic support for action against Iran with extreme statements that he knew would soon be contradicted by his own intelligence agencies. Yet this is precisely what Bush did.

Ironically, the NIE's conclusion that Iran did not have a nuclear weapons program did not change the undisputed fact that it does have a uranium enrichment program that allows it to produce the fissile material for nuclear weapons, which is the most difficult hurdle in the atom bomb–making process. Bush's reckless rhetoric severely undercut his ability to gather support to deal with this still real problem.

The NIE concluded that Iran had halted its nuclear weapons program in 2003 because it feared international isolation:

> Tehran's decision to halt its nuclear weapons program suggests it is less determined to develop nuclear weapons than we have been judging since 2005. Our assessment that the program probably was halted primarily in response to international pressure suggests Iran may be more vulnerable to influence on the issue than we judged previously.

This punctured the image of Iran as a country of mad mullahs bent on acquiring nuclear weapons that they might use in a suicidal mission against the United States or Israel. Implicit in this analysis of Iran's behavior is that Iran is a rational actor open to a deal that enhanced its security and acknowledged its role as an important regional power.

Some of the administration's other charges against Iran defy common sense. In his Reno speech in August 2007, President Bush accused Iran of arming the Taliban in Afghanistan while his administration has, at various times, accused Iran of giving weapons to both Sunni and Shiite insurgents in Iraq. The Taliban are Salafi jihadis, Sunni fundamentalists who consider Shiites apostates deserving of death. In power, the Taliban brutally repressed Afghanistan's Shiites and nearly provoked a war with Iran when they murdered Iranian diplomats inside the Iranian consulate in the northern city of Mazar-i-Sharif. The Iranians and their allies in Afghanistan are opposed to the recrudescent Taliban, not sympathetic to it.

Iraq's Sunni insurgents are either Salafi jihadis or Baathists, the political party that started the Iran–Iraq War. The Iranian regime may believe it has a strategic interest in keeping US forces tied down in the Iraqi quagmire since this, in the Iranian view, makes an attack on Iran unlikely. US clashes with Moqtada al-Sadr's Mahdi Army complicate the American military effort in Iraq and it is plausible that Iran might provide some weapons—including armor-penetrating IEDs—to the Mahdi Army and its splinter factions. Overall, however, Iran has no interest in the success of the Mahdi Army. Al-Sadr has made Iraqi nationalism his political platform. He has attacked the SIIC for its pro-Iranian leanings and challenged Iraq's most important religious figure, Ayatollah Sistani, himself an Iranian citizen. Asked about charges that Iran was organizing Iraqi insurgents, Iran's Deputy Foreign Minister Abbas Araghchi told *The Financial Times* on May 10, 2007, "The whole idea is unreasonable. Why should we do that? Why should we undermine a government in Iraq that we support more than anybody else?"

The United States cannot now undo President Bush's strategic gift to Iran. But importantly, the most pro-Iranian Shiite political party is the one least hostile to the United States. In the battle now underway between the SIIC and Moqtada al-Sadr for control of southern Iraq and of the central government in Baghdad, the United States and Iran are on the same side. The US has good reason to worry about Iran's activities in Iraq. But contrary to the Bush administration's allegations—supported by both General David Petraeus and Ambassador Ryan Crocker in their recent congressional testimony—Iran does not oppose Iraq's new political order. In fact, Iran is the major beneficiary of the American-induced changes that have taken place in Iraq since 2003.

—January 18, 2008

# 5

## BUSH'S AMAZING ACHIEVEMENT

### *Jonathan Freedland*

ONE OF THE few foreign policy achievements of the Bush administration has been the creation of a near consensus among those who study international affairs, a shared view that stretches, however improbably, from Noam Chomsky to Brent Scowcroft, from the antiwar protesters on the streets of San Francisco to the well-upholstered office of former secretary of state James Baker. This new consensus holds that the 2003 invasion of Iraq was a calamity, that the presidency of George W. Bush has reduced America's standing in the world and made the United States less, not more, secure, leaving its enemies emboldened and its friends alienated. Paid-up members of the nation's foreign policy establishment, those who have held some of the most senior offices in the land, speak in a language once confined to the T-shirts of placard-wielding demonstrators. They rail against deception and dishonesty, imperialism and corruption. The only dispute between them is over the size and depth of the hole into which Bush has led the country he pledged to serve.

The December 2006 Baker-Hamilton report, drawn up by a bipartisan panel of ten Washington eminences with perhaps a couple of centuries of national security experience between them and not a radical bone in their collective body, described the mess the Bush team had left in Iraq as "grave and deteriorating." The seventy-nine

recommendations they made amounted to a demand that the administration repudiate its entire policy and start again. In the words of former congressman Lee Hamilton, James Baker's co-chair and a rock-solid establishment figure, "Our ship of state has hit rough waters. It must now chart a new way forward."[1]

So it comes as less of a surprise than once it might have to see Dennis Ross, in *Statecraft and How to Restore America's Standing in the World*,[2] and Zbigniew Brzezinski, in *Second Chance: Three Presidents and the Crisis of American Superpower*[3]—two further fixtures of the national security elite—step forward to slam the administration in terms that would, in an earlier era, have seemed uncouth for men of their rank. Neither Ross, who served as Middle East envoy for both George H.W. Bush and Bill Clinton, nor Brzezinski, a conservative Democrat and cold war hawk, could be dismissed as *Nation*-reading, Howard Dean types. Yet in withering new books they both eviscerate the Bush record, writing in the tone of exasperated elders who handed over the family business to a new generation, only to see their successors drive the firm into bankruptcy. Both books offer rescue plans for a US foreign policy they consider to be in tatters.

Accordingly, their arguments are less striking than the fact that it is Ross and Brzezinski who are making them. Those who have been listening to the antiwar movement since 2002 will nod along at this assessment of the Iraq adventure:

> It is hard to exaggerate the Bush administration's fundamental miscalculations on Iraq, including but not limited to unrealistic policy objectives; fundamental intelligence failures; catastroph-

---

1. "Iraq Report Well Received in Washington," NPR, December 6, 2006, available at www.npr.org/templates/story/story.php?storyId=6587217.

2. Farrar, Straus and Giroux, 2007.

3. Basic Books, 2007.

ically poor understanding of what would characterize the post-Saddam period, and completely unrealistic planning as a result; denial of the existence of an insurgency for several months; and the absence of a consistent explanation to the American people or the international community about the reasons for the war.

Small wonder that after nearly four years of warfare, Iraq has been a disaster, costing thousands of lives, requiring the expenditure of hundreds of billions of dollars, stretching our forces and reserve system to the breaking point, and becoming a magnet for terrorists and hostility toward the United States throughout the Muslim world.

But they should marvel that it comes from Dennis Ross, a loyal former lieutenant of Baker's who writes glowingly of Bush *père* and who was as comfortable in a Republican administration as a Democratic one. If they do not, then it is only because Chuck Hagel, Gordon Smith, Scowcroft, and even the late Gerald Ford have made Republican attacks on the Bush record since 2001 seem normal.

Similarly, a sentence like this has been uttered in European chancelleries every week for five years:

> The Iraq War in all its aspects has turned into a calamity—in the way it was internally decided, externally promoted, and has been conducted—and it has already stamped the Bush presidency as a historical failure.

Yet that verdict comes not from some Venusian in Paris or Berlin but from Brzezinksi, that hardheaded Martian creature of Washington. Lest there be any doubt, the former national security adviser to Jimmy Carter issues a report card on the three presidencies since the end of the cold war. George H.W. Bush gets a B, praised for his calm management of the expiration of the Soviet Union and the united

international front he constructed for his own desert confrontation with Saddam. Clinton manages a C, credited for effective championing of globalization and oversight of NATO enlargement, but debited for allowing too many important matters, especially nuclear proliferation, to drift. Bush's son is slapped with an unambiguous F.

That verdict is rooted in the administration's invasion and occupation of Iraq, which can't help but form the heart of both books. Judged even by the lights of Bush's own "war on terror" it has been a spectacular failure. It took a country that had been free of jihadist militants and turned it into their most fecund breeding ground; it took a country that posed no threat to the United States and made it into a place where thousands of Americans, not to mention many tens, if not hundreds, of thousands of Iraqis, have been killed. And it diverted resources from the task that should have been uppermost after September 11, namely the hunting down of Osama bin Laden and his top lieutenants, allowing them to slip out of reach.

What's more, Bush's "war on terror" did bin Laden's work for him. Brzezinksi is not alone in suggesting that it was a mistake to treat September 11 as an act of war, rather than as an outrageous crime; in so doing, the administration endowed al-Qaeda with the status it craved. What followed was a series of missteps that seemed bent on vindicating the jihadists' claim of a war of the West against Islam. Whether it was the invasion of Iraq or the early talk of a "crusade" or the abuses at Guantánamo Bay and Abu Ghraib, the Bush administration fed violent Islamism all it needed to recruit young men the world over. What began as a fringe sect has become, thanks in no small measure to the Bush administration, a global movement able to draw on deep wells of support.

There were ancillary effects. North Korea and Iran, in addition to Saddam Hussein's Iraq the other two charter members of the axis of evil, became more dangerous in the Bush years, advancing further down the nuclear road. That was partly because, with the US tied down in Iraq, they were given a free hand; and partly because the

thumping of Saddam had taught would-be nuclear powers a crucial lesson. As Ross puts it, "We attacked Iraq, which did not have nuclear weapons, but have avoided doing the same with the North Koreans, who may have as many as twelve." The 2003 invasion served as a glossy advertisement for the protective power of nuclear arms.

Both Ross and Brzezinski reserve special contempt for Bush's handling of the Israeli–Palestinian conflict, shifting the US position from that of an honest broker, albeit one sympathetic to one side, to a partisan ready to indulge whatever course Israel chose to adopt. Here Ross draws on his experience as Middle East envoy during the years of the Oslo peace process, explaining how disengagement by the Bush administration has not only prevented progress but also actively aggravated the conflict. Both authors lay out how the administration's refusal to undertake the hard work of peacemaking has deprived the Palestinians of the state they have craved so long, denied Israel the long-term security it needs, and allowed the sore that most poisons Muslim attitudes toward the West to fester.

For those with the stamina to face it, there are further indictments in both books of every aspect of US foreign policy, from the failure to take a lead on dealing with climate change to the distracted inattention to the rise of China. Some of these strategic blunders relate once again to the invasion of Iraq, whether it be the needless estrangement of European allies or the avoidable driving into a corner of Iran, whose influence from Baghdad to Beirut has self-evidently increased.

The accumulated result has been a plunge in global esteem for the United States. A survey in January 2007 for the BBC World Service found that only 29 percent of those polled in eighteen countries believed the US was playing a "mainly positive role in the world," a fall of eleven points in two years.[4] As Brzezinski writes,

---

4. "World View of US Role Goes from Bad to Worse," available at www.publicdiplomacy.org/14.htm#Apr2007.

> Because of Bush's self-righteously unilateral conduct of US foreign policy after 9/11, the evocative symbol of America in the eyes of much of the world ceased to be the Statue of Liberty and instead became the Guantánamo prison camp.

It's hard to read Ross and Brzezinksi without coming to share their nostalgia for the steady, realistic, and grounded statecraft of George H. W. Bush in contrast with the faith-based pursuit of neoconservative fantasy that has passed for international affairs under his son.

Scathing as they are, these books are mere slaps on the wrist compared to *Nemesis*,[5] the third volume in Chalmers Johnson's blistering trilogy, which stands as the centerpiece of the American Empire Project, a series of works published by Metropolitan Books examining recent changes in America's strategic thinking, particularly under the Bush administration, and the consequences of those changes at home and abroad. The first in Johnson's series, *Blowback: The Costs and Consequences of American Empire*, argued that the United States had, particularly through the covert activities of the Central Intelligence Agency, spilled so much blood and caused so much damage in other people's countries that it was only a matter of time before it felt the wrath of those nations' vengeance. (The term "blowback," Johnson concedes, was not his own coinage: the CIA used it following its involvement in the 1953 overthrow of Iran's elected prime minister, Mohammad Mossadeq, an event that, according to Johnson, led to the blowback of the 1979 revolution and the installation by Ayatollah Ruhollah Khomeini of the anti-American theocracy which has ruled ever since.) *Blowback* was published in March 2000, making little impact. It took only eighteen months, however, for *Blowback* suddenly to look chillingly prescient, winning an audience for Johnson he might otherwise have lacked.

---

5. *Nemesis: The Last Days of the American Republic* (Metropolitan, 2006).

For while Brzezinski in particular edges up to the outer limits of the Washington foreign policy consensus, Johnson unabashedly stands far outside it. Ross and Brzezinski, as former security officials, take as their premise the belief that the United States should be the dominant force in international relations; Brzezinski goes so far as to dub Bush, Clinton, and Bush as "Global Leader" I, II, and III. The chief complaint of both Brzezinski and Ross is that the current president has fumbled this designated role. Johnson's starting point is quite different: he brands as imperial arrogance the very assumption that America should extend its reach across the planet (and beyond, into the heavens).

The clue is in the subtitle: "The Last Days of the American Republic." Johnson joins those who urge Americans, despite their anti-imperial origins in ejecting King George, to see that they have succeeded both ancient Rome and nineteenth-century Britain in becoming the empire of their age. This impulse became fashionable in the post–September 11 period, including among those who saw the imperial mission in a benign light.[6] Johnson's perspective is very different. He wants the scales to fall from American eyes so that the nation can see the truth about its role in the world, a truth he finds ugly.

Scholars can make a parlor game of compare and contrast between Washington and Rome, and the parallels are indeed striking.[7] Both rank as the predominant military powers of their time, Rome brooking no competition, while, by Johnson's reckoning, US military spending exceeds that of all the other defense budgets on earth combined. In each case, military strength both fosters and is fostered by technological prowess: while Roman armies built the straight roads that

---

6. See, among others, Michael Ignatieff, "The Burden," *The New York Times Magazine*, January 5, 2003; and Niall Ferguson, *Colossus: The Price of America's Empire* (Penguin, 2004).

7. See, for the most recent example, Cullen Murphy, *Are We Rome? The Fall of an Empire and the Fate of America* (Houghton Mifflin, 2007).

served as the arteries of their conquered lands, so the US Department of Defense incubated the information superhighway, the Internet that now girdles the globe.

The Romans often preferred to exercise power through friendly client regimes, rather than direct rule: until Jay Garner and L. Paul Bremer became US proconsuls in Baghdad, that was the American method too. Rome even took in the scions of their defeated peoples' leading families, the better to prepare them for their future as Rome's puppets; perhaps comparable are Washington's elite private schools, full of the "pro-Western" Arab kings, South American presidents, and African leaders of the future. Sometimes the approach backfired, then and now. Several of those who rebelled against Rome had earlier been sponsored as pliant allies; their contemporary counterparts would surely be Saddam Hussein, a former US ally against Iran, and Osama bin Laden, who in his earlier career in the anti-Soviet resistance in Afghanistan benefited, if indirectly, from CIA largesse. (In his book *Taliban: Militant Islam, Oil and Fundamentalism in Central Asia* (2000), the journalist Ahmed Rashid writes that in 1986, bin Laden "helped build the Khost tunnel complex, which the CIA was funding as a major arms storage depot, training facility, and medical center for the Mujaheddin, deep under the mountains close to the Pakistan border." Rashid quotes bin Laden as telling Agence France-Presse that at that time "I set up my first camp where... volunteers were trained by Pakistani and American officers. The weapons were supplied by the Americans, the money by the Saudis.")

Still, Johnson is in deadly earnest when he draws a parallel with Rome. He swats aside the conventional objection that, in contrast with both Romans and Britons, Americans have never constructed colonies abroad. Oh, but they have, he says; it's just that Americans are blind to them. America is an "empire of bases," he writes, with a network of vast, hardened military encampments across the earth, each one a match for any Roman or Raj outpost. Official figures speak of 737 US military bases in foreign countries, adding up to an

armed American presence, whether large or small, in 132 of the 190 member states of the United Nations.

Johnson reckons the number is actually higher, if one includes those bases about which the Pentagon is coy. The 2005 *Base Structure Report* omits to mention, for example, garrisons in Kosovo, as well as bases in Afghanistan, Iraq, Israel, Kyrgyzstan, Qatar, and Uzbekistan, even though it is well known that the US established a vast presence in both the Persian Gulf and Central Asia after September 11. (Admittedly, the US was evicted from its base in Uzbekistan in 2005.) Nor does the Pentagon ledger include the extensive military and espionage installations it maintains in Britain, estimated to be worth some $5 billion, since these are nominally facilities of the Royal Air Force. "If there were an honest account, the actual size of our military empire would probably top 1,000 different bases overseas, but no-one—possibly not even the Pentagon—knows the exact number for sure," writes Johnson. Intriguingly, he notes that the thirty-eight large and medium-sized US facilities around the world, mostly air and naval bases, match almost exactly both the thirty-six naval bases and army garrisons Britain maintained at its imperial peak in 1898 and the thirty-seven major sites used by the Romans to police the empire from Britannia to Egypt, Hispania to Armenia in 117 AD. "Perhaps," muses Johnson, "the optimum number of major citadels and fortresses for an imperialist aspiring to dominate the world is somewhere between thirty-five and forty."

Precise figures are hard to come by, but there are an estimated 325,000 US military personnel deployed abroad, often alongside dependents and large numbers of civilians, most of them living in sealed compounds, each one a little island of America. As Johnson showed in his 2004 book, *The Sorrows of Empire*, this is a parallel world that has its own airline, the Air Mobility Command, connecting one base to another, and an elaborate system, known as Morale, Welfare, and Recreation (MWR), dedicated to ensuring that America's imperial servants feel they have never left home. They can be entertained in

their own multiplexes playing the latest blockbusters, amused by satellite television airing American shows, and fed by fully stocked branches of Burger King. Johnson spares no detail:

> Some of the "rest-and-recreation" facilities include the armed forces ski center at Garmisch in the Bavarian Alps, over two hundred military golf courses around the world, some seventy-one Learjets and other luxury aircraft to fly admirals and generals to such watering holes, and luxury hotels for our troops and their families in Tokyo, Seoul, on the Italian Riviera, at Florida's Disney World, and many other places.

The most recent addition to the empire is perhaps the most arresting. The new US embassy in Baghdad is, despite its name, a base. It is set inside a 104-acre compound, making it "six times larger than the UN, as big as Vatican City, and costing $592 million to build." It will be defended by blast walls and ground-to-air missiles, and have its own apartment buildings, along with its own electricity, water supply, and sewage system. (In a dry aside, Johnson notes that "like the former American embassy in Saigon, the Baghdad embassy will have one or more helipads on the roofs.") Life will continue here as it already goes on in the US-enforced Green Zone, complete with its swimming pools, dry-cleaning outlets, and around-the-clock availability of pork in the mess canteen, as cosseted and disconnected from the surrounding reality as Happy Valley was from the rest of Kenya.[8]

Johnson argues this point in the same way he presents his entire case, through the accumulation of cold numbers and hard facts. Little of his material is drawn from primary research; rather Johnson scours published sources and draws facts together to form a picture few oth-

---

8. For a breathtaking account of the American enclave in Baghdad, see Rajiv Chandrasekaran, *Imperial Life in the Emerald City: Inside Iraq's Green Zone* (Knopf, 2006).

ers are willing to see. He doesn't labor the imperial analogies, but the similarities are clear. While Rome used to tax its colonies, the US expects those who host American bases to do their bit for "burden sharing," paying for their own protection, as it were. Japan pays up most: $4.4 billion in 2002. These arrangements are presented as voluntary, but Johnson is skillful at showing how, stage by stage, the host countries have little hope of showing their American guests the door.

In some respects, the parallel with the British Empire is the more striking, with the defeated and therefore reliable nations of Japan and Germany playing the role Britain once assigned to its dominions in South Africa or New Zealand. More importantly, the British told themselves to the very end that they were only ruling other parts of the world, painting the map pink, from the noblest of intentions. Their goal was to bring civilization to the dark continents, their rhetorical fervor no less than the Americans of today who swear their sole purpose is the export of democracy.

Some, even among American foreign policy's sternest critics, accept that self-description. William Pfaff has recently written that today's Americans, like the British before them, are engaged in something other than crude, acquisitive imperialism. If that was their goal, if Iraq really was all about oil, as many in the antiwar movement have long insisted, then the US could simply have annexed the relevant areas and installed a dictator. But Pfaff argues that the American purpose is of a different order. While "empires usually leave their subjects as they find them," he wrote, "colonizers want to teach new values, convert the hearts and—so to speak—save the souls of the colonized." Iraq has been, wrote Pfaff, an exercise in "value conversion," seeking to win the country for Western-style government and market capitalism.[9]

---

9. "The Doomed Colonial Wars of the US and NATO," March 2, 2007, available at www .williampfaff.com/modules/news/article.php?storyid=212.

I suspect that Chalmers Johnson would snort at the notion that Americans are well-meaning colonizers, set only on saving the souls of their subject peoples. For Johnson, the talk of value conversion is only so much fluff, designed to win the public support that would be absent for a naked smash-and-grab raid on a sovereign state. All imperial adventures have disguised themselves as civilizing missions; even the Spanish conquistadors of the sixteenth century claimed to be freeing from superstition and backwardness the Aztec, Mayan, and Inca peoples they crushed. In this reading, the rhetoric is only rhetoric. America's purpose is the same as imperialism's ever was, to allow the foreign power safe and unimpeded access to whatever pickings the plundered nation has to offer.

What complicates the picture is the sincerity, naive as it may be, of so many of those neoconservative dreamers, perhaps extending to the President himself. Clearly they, no less than their British predecessors, believe, or believed, that they are engaged in the work of liberation rather than conquest. Are they themselves deceived by shadowy forces who use the veneer of spreading democracy to conceal a more base purpose? Or is it instead that imperialism, once in motion, exerts a momentum of its own?

While they often converge on the same point, Johnson enters this discussion from an angle different from that of Noam Chomsky and the traditional anti-imperialist left. He certainly has sympathy for those who have found themselves on the receiving end of America's sense of manifest destiny, including the luckless Japanese who have had to endure the boorishness and sometimes outright brutality of the 50,000 US troops, military-related civilians, and their dependents stationed in Okinawa. But his is a patriot's passion: his motive is to save the American republic he loves. While Chomsky argues that American guilt can be traced back to the Constitution—he disapprovingly quotes James Madison's insistence that the new republic

should "protect the minority of the opulent against the majority"[10]—Johnson reveres that document and the careful balance of powers it constructed. His fear is that America's steady descent into imperialism renders those arrangements unsustainable, just as the rise of the Roman Empire ensured the slow death of the Roman Republic.

This is the core of his argument, that by extending its reach in the world America is not only endangering itself physically, by increasing the risk of blowback, but bankrupting itself, financially, constitutionally, and morally. The economic evidence is devastating, a succession of numbers each more stark than the last. The annual Pentagon budget, which falls short of $500 billion, is far from the whole story. There are also the separately accounted costs of the wars in Iraq and Afghanistan, which stood in 2006 at approximately $450 billion since their inception. When those sums are combined with military spending by agencies other than the Pentagon, the national defense outlay for 2007 reaches $622 billion. Johnson would have us add to that figure the ongoing costs of wars past, including the lifetime care of the seriously wounded ($68 billion) and widows' pensions, as well as State Department subsidies paid to foreign countries to encourage their purchase of US-made weapons ($23 billion). That would still exclude the interest paid on the share of the national debt incurred by military spending, for which Johnson cites one estimate of $138.7 billion. Even on the most conservative reckoning, the US is spending more in real terms on defense now than at any time since the Second World War. If it accounts for a relatively modest share of GDP, perhaps less than 5 percent, that is only because the US economy is now so much bigger than it was.[11]

What's driving this is a nexus of military, political, and financial

---

10. See Noam Chomsky, *Failed States: The Abuse of Power and the Assault on Democracy* (Metropolitan, 2006), p. 207.

11. Much of the publicly available data on military spending is gathered by the Center for Strategic and Budgetary Assessments, www.csbaonline.org.

interests, all of whom benefit from ever-increasing military spending. Johnson provides an anatomy of one particularly egregious example, the expansion into space weaponry represented by the so-called National Missile Defense program (NMD). Patiently he demonstrates why a system aimed at intercepting nuclear bombs before they can land on America does not and could not work. For one thing, no one has yet worked out how to identify a hostile launch and no interceptor has yet been designed that can tell the difference between an incoming warhead and a decoy. The result is that NMD is nothing more than a boondoggle in the sky, at last count pulling in $130 billion of American taxpayers' money, a figure which on current plans would reach $1.2 trillion by 2015.

But the NMD pork-in-space project is far from exceptional. Seeking fat contracts, the big defense companies give donations to those politicians who will pay them back by commissioning expensive defense projects; the contractors then reward the politicians by locating their firms in their districts; finally the voters, glad of the jobs, reward the politicians by reelecting them. Johnson offers dozens of examples, including Florida's Democratic senator Bill Nelson, a member of the Armed Services Committee, who in the 2006 federal budget "obtained $916 million for defense projects, about two-thirds of which went to the Florida-based plants of Boeing, Honeywell, General Dynamics, Armor Holdings, and other munitions makers." Since 2003, Nelson has received $108,750 in campaign contributions from thirteen companies for which he arranged contracts. It's a cycle perpetuated by everyone involved: contractors, politicians, voters. Everyone benefits from this untamed form of military Keynesianism—except the next generations of Americans who can be expected to drown in a debt that now measures $9 trillion and grows daily.

Yet even this does not pose the greatest danger to the republic. Johnson looks to Rome and to Caesar to demonstrate how the powers required to maintain an empire are incompatible with the checks and balances of a republic. His attempts to argue this theoretically are

weaker than his practical case studies. He describes in detail the CIA's transformation from Harry Truman's provider of reliable intelligence into an outfit that performs covert military operations—such as the toppling of Chile's democratically elected president Salvador Allende in the 1973 coup which installed the murderous regime of Augusto Pinochet. The CIA, writes Johnson, has long been beyond the reach of meaningful democratic oversight; it has become a presidential private army, an American counterpart to Rome's praetorian guard.

Tellingly, however, his most powerful evidence is drawn from the Bush years since 2001. Johnson may argue that these are trends that have been in evidence for decades, but it is the current administration which has illuminated them. By declaring the nation at war and himself a war-time president, Bush has grabbed powers to himself that America's founders never intended him to have. As the infamous "torture memo" made clear, Bush's legal team has constructed something it calls the "unitary executive theory of the presidency" to place the Oval Office outside the law, arguing that there can be no infringement on his "ulti-mate authority" as commander in chief in the conduct of war. Because practically any measures taken, at home or abroad, since September 11, 2001, can be construed as the conduct of war, this doctrine is nothing less than a claim of absolute power. Whether it be treaties signed and ratified by the US, like the Geneva Conventions, or the laws of the land passed in Congress, nothing can touch him. He is Caesar.

There was a time when such claims would have sounded over-heated (and some, like Johnson's comparison of Bush, Dick Cheney, and Donald Rumsfeld to Adolf Eichmann, still do). Yet now Johnson finds mainstream allies for at least part of his case, Brzezinski among them. Not only is Brzezinski unafraid to describe US activities as imperial, he has joined those who believe the current administration is "propagating fear and paranoia" and is engaged in "the deliberate manipulation of public anxiety." Once again, this was the sort of argument previously marshaled chiefly by those outside the United

States and a world away from its governing circles.[12] It testifies to Bush's recklessness that he has now placed a man of Brzezinski's stature alongside them.

With the license granted by the "war on terror," and the acquiescence of both Congress (until January 2007) and much of the US press and television, as well as several federal judges, the administration has been able to trample on the Constitution and the once-cherished liberties it contains. The pattern is clear, whether it involves eavesdropping without a warrant by the National Security Agency; the denial of habeas corpus to inmates of Guantánamo Bay; the deliberate obstruction of the Freedom of Information Act; the constant use of presidential "signing statements" usually to nullify legislation passed by both houses of Congress and signed by the President himself; or the torture at Abu Ghraib and Camp X-Ray. As Johnson writes:

> Over any fairly lengthy period of time, successful imperialism requires that a domestic republic or a domestic democracy change into a domestic tyranny.... The United States today, like the Roman Republic in the first century BC, is threatened by an out-of-control military-industrial complex and a huge secret government controlled exclusively by the president. After the attacks of September 11, 2001, cynical and short-sighted political leaders of the United States began to enlarge the powers of the president at the expense of the elected representatives of the people and the courts.

The public went along, accepting the excuse that a little tyranny was

---

12. See the BBC TV documentary *The Power of Nightmares*, written and produced by Adam Curtis, 2004. It argued that politicians who could no longer inspire sought to scare instead, citing the Bush team as a prime example. "Instead of delivering dreams, politicians now promise to protect us: from nightmares," the film's introduction declares. It has never been shown on American television.

necessary to protect the population. But, as Benjamin Franklin wrote in 1759, "Those who would give up essential liberty to purchase a little temporary safety deserve neither liberty nor safety."

What can be done? For Ross and Brzezinski, the solutions are arduous, but at least imaginable. Ross urges a return to statecraft, to the painstaking work of diplomacy and alliance building. Indeed, of the three books, his is the one that would be of most direct use to the next administration taking office in 2009. Condoleezza Rice's successor could do worse than sit down with Ross's "Negotiation: Twelve Rules to Follow," followed by his "Eleven Rules for Mediation." (A canny publisher might try to publish those sections on their own, aiming them at the CEO market; inside Ross's foreign policy monograph there may be a business best-seller crying to get out.)

Among his concrete tips is the suggestion that the US back a new nongovernmental body to perform, under international direction and in secular fashion, the popular tasks now undertaken by the Islamists of Hamas or Hezbollah, namely providing social services and building civic institutions like hospitals and schools. Ross surely sees the danger of such an approach: that any agency known to be US-backed would instantly be deemed suspect by much of the Palestinian street. His answer might be to seek Saudi, rather than American, patronage, exploiting Riyadh's palpable anxiety over the rise of Iran and its Islamist proxies in Gaza and Lebanon. The Saudis, Ross argues, could be persuaded to bankroll anti-Islamist forces, including the Fatah party of Palestinian president Mahmoud Abbas, if that would weaken Hamas.

Ross is right to see the opportunity presented by Sunni concern over the rise of Iran, an opportunity to form an alliance against aggressive Islamism that the Bush administration has squandered. Still, one cannot help but detect a bad, even imperialist habit here: the desire to pick other nations' representatives for them. Rather than

devising clever ruses to marginalize Hamas, would not US energies be better spent encouraging Hamas toward a political, rather than armed, pursuit of its goals, dangling before the organization the rewards that would come if it changed course?

Ross has some imaginative ideas for Iran, too, including an alternative to full-scale military action. He floats the notion of a covert operation to sabotage Iran's delicate nuclear machinery. Such a step, he writes cheerfully, would "prove very costly for the Iranians to overcome, and yet would be completely deniable." Unlike Bush's former UN ambassador John Bolton, who said, "I don't do carrots," Ross is keen to show he would use both the carrots of "soft power" and the sticks of physical force as well. One wonders, though, how "deniable" such force could be in today's world and if such a covert plan could be efficiently executed in the first place.

Brzezinski is equally brimming with advice, calling, like Ross, for a Washington that shows more respect to the world and one that would shore up the Euro-Atlantic area of nations, lest it lose its influence to East Asia. Most radically, he advocates for a shift in the American social model, away from excess consumption and income inequality toward a more ecologically sustainable pattern that would appeal internationally. One of Brzezinski's most striking observations is that an "awakening" is underway around the world, a stirring, if vague, sense of injustice—and that the United States can only succeed if it is held to be on the right side of the divide. "In today's restless world, America needs to identify itself with the quest for universal human dignity," he writes. What that will take, he adds provocatively, is both "a cultural revolution and regime change."

Necessarily, it is Johnson, who has diagnosed a more radical problem, who has to come up with a more radical solution. He cannot merely call for greater powers for Congress, because by his own lights, "the legislative branch of our government is broken," reduced to the supine creature of large corporations, the defense contractors first

among them. Instead, he urges a surge in direct democracy, "a grass-roots movement to abolish the CIA, break the hold of the military-industrial complex, and establish public financing of elections"—but he has the grace to recognize how unlikely such a development is.

So he is left offering not an eleven- or twelve-step program, but rather a historical choice. Either the United States can follow the lead of the Romans, who chose to keep their empire and so lost their republic. Or "we could, like the British Empire after World War II, keep our democracy by giving up our empire." That choice was neither smooth nor executed heroically, but it was the right one. Now much of the world watches the offspring of that empire, nearly two and a half centuries later—hoping it makes the same choice, and trembling at the prospect that it might not.

—May 17, 2007

POSTSCRIPT

While the Ross and Brzezinski view of the Bush record has, if anything, become even more mainstream since the time of writing, Chalmers Johnson's more radical critique of US foreign policy remains firmly outside the conventional wisdom. In the early stages of the 2008 presidential campaign, for example, while Barack Obama, John Edwards, and Hillary Clinton competed to show off their willingness to stand against the Bush administration, it fell to a Republican routinely described as a maverick, Representative Ron Paul of Texas, to offer anything that came close to Johnson's analysis. In the CNN/YouTube Republican debate on November 28, 2007, Paul railed not only against the Iraq war but the entire drift of US imperialistic foreign policy, planting its bases all over the world: "I don't want to send troops overseas using force to tell [other people] how to live. We would object to it here and they're going to object to us over there." Paul's willingness to speak in terms that echo Johnson's attack

on American "hubris" may not have won him many early votes, but it helped build a small but remarkably dedicated following for the congressman—proof, perhaps, that there is some appetite for such ideas on both the American left and right.

—January 6, 2008

# 6

## CRACKS IN THE HOUSE OF ROVE

### *Jonathan Raban*

LIKE SO MANY parties that go on past their proper bedtime, Karl Rove's Republican Party has lately begun to break out in fights, as neocon theorists, Goldwater-style libertarians, the corporations, and grassroots Christian fundamentalists come to the aggravating discovery that they're more defined by their differences than by what they hold in common. On climate change, government spending, stem-cell research, reproductive rights, and the Iraq war, to name just a few of the triggering issues, self-styled conservatives find themselves at loggerheads with other self-styled conservatives, each claiming the mantle of true conservatism for himself. As both symptom and diagnosis of this interesting—one might say promising—development, Andrew Sullivan's *The Conservative Soul* is as engaging as it is provocative.[1]

Sullivan is an odd duck. Born in England in 1963 to an Irish immigrant family, he grew up in East Grinstead, a town long associated with a choleric, class-based brand of reactionary Toryism. Whenever letters appeared in the *Daily Telegraph* demanding the return of the birch or the noose, the chances were good that they'd be signed by Colonel Blimp (retd.) of East Grinstead, Sussex. But that was never Sullivan's style of conservatism. A beneficiary (as I was) of the 1944

---

*The Conservative Soul: How We Lost It, How to Get It Back* (HarperCollins, 2006).

Education Act, he passed the eleven-plus exam and went to Reigate Grammar School, where he became a "teenage Thatcherite" and sported a Reagan button in 1980. From there, he won a scholarship to Oxford, becoming the first member of his family to attend university. He was elected president of the Oxford Union and, in 1983, or so he has boasted, threw a champagne party to celebrate the arrival of Pershing II missiles in Britain. An exemplary product of British meritocracy, he went on to Harvard, where he completed a Ph.D. with a dissertation on the British conservative thinker Michael Oakeshott. Its title, "Intimations Pursued: The Voice of Practice in the Conversation of Michael Oakeshott," played on the title of Oakeshott's 1959 essay "The Voice of Poetry in the Conversation of Mankind."

As someone committed—almost, it seems, from the cradle—to minimal government, maximal personal liberty, and a "strong anti-communist foreign policy," Sullivan's natural habitat was the United States. In the 1990s he was the youngest-ever editor of *The New Republic*; he is now a blogger, columnist, and ubiquitous guest on radio and cable TV talk shows, where he speaks in a peculiar creole, half English, half American, an accent from a region located somewhere on the sea floor of the Atlantic, midway between the Azores and Flemish Cap. This highly idiosyncratic mongrel voice tells one something about the character of Sullivan's conservative journey, on which he has been, variously, Irish among the English, a scholarship boy among the sons and daughters of privilege, an Englishman among Americans, an HIV-positive gay man among right-wing homophobes, and a liberal Catholic among fundamentalists—good training for a chameleon, as for a combative gadfly, and Sullivan is both. Along the way, he's fallen out with most of his political fellow travelers, most recently with the Bush administration and all its works. In *The Conservative Soul* he summons to his aid a trinity of mentors—Oakeshott, Christ, and Montaigne—to explain his furious disillusion with the presidency he once extolled.

Sullivan makes plain that his singular view of the world was both confirmed and shaped by Oakeshott's writing, and in figuring out Sullivan it helps to know something of his intellectual hero. In conservative circles, Oakeshott (1901–1990) is often said to be the greatest English political philosopher since Hobbes, and is widely credited with having been the gray eminence behind Thatcherism. It's most unlikely that Margaret Thatcher ever read him, but Sir Keith Joseph, the token intellectual in her cabinet, was at least on nodding terms with both the man and his work.

Central to Oakeshott's thought was his conviction that reality consists in the unending swarm and confluence of intractable particulars and contingencies. So historians, reading the past backward from the present, impose on it illicit patterns dictated by their contemporary concerns, while politicians project on the future equally vain patterns in the form of grand schemes for the improvement of humankind. Oakeshott's great abomination was what he called Rationalism (always with a capital R and with the emphasis on the ism), the dominant force, as he saw it, in Western politics since the Enlightenment, and the source of every collectivist attempt to build utopia by reasoning on the basis of "felt needs."

By this measure, the framers of the American Constitution, Marx, Engels, and Hitler were all Rationalists, and Oakeshott's catch-all list of dangerous Rationalist projects included the "so-called Re-Union of the Christian churches," "the destruction of the Austro-Hungarian Empire," "the World State (of H. G. Wells or anyone else)," the Beveridge Report (blueprint for Britain's postwar welfare state), the 1944 Education Act, and "the revival of Gaelic as the official language of Eire." What on earth would he have made, one wonders, of the neoconservative Project for the New American Century? "The conjunction of ruling and dreaming generates tyranny," Oakeshott wrote, and he likened the proper role of government to that of an umpire, there to ensure that the rules of the game are observed. In the

ideal Oakeshottian world, as nearly all history would be shelved under Myth and Legend, so government would be conspicuous by its absence except when required to arbitrate on disputed line calls.

Oakeshott is a severe and witty critic of both history and politics, though it's hard to imagine a practicing historian or politician reading him without suffering from an attack of extreme and paralyzing self-consciousness. For conservative political journalists like Sullivan, though, he's a natural touchstone—a skeptic's skeptic, who sets a standard of Olympian minimalism against which to calibrate governmental excesses. In *The Conservative Soul*, Oakeshott's ghost is summoned as the first prosecution witness against the Bush administration's conduct of the war in Iraq, its fiscal extravagance, and its doctrinaire refusal to recognize gay marriage as a de facto reality of our time.

What is baffling is why such an ardent disciple of Oakeshott came to sign himself up for the Bush program in the first place—a decision that Sullivan now says he finds "more than a little worrying." For, from the moment of its declaration, the "war on terror" ("this crusade," as Bush then defined it), by committing the United States to an indefinite future of hostilities against a shadowy and shape-shifting enemy, had all the hallmarks of one of Oakeshott's most deluded Rationalist projects. Yet even as Osama bin Laden morphed into Saddam Hussein, and Paul Wolfowitz unrolled his great plan for the democratization of the Middle East by force of arms, Sullivan was a raucous cheerleader for the administration.

On September 11, 2001, Sullivan described the attacks on the World Trade Center and the Pentagon as "the single most devastating act of war since Nagasaki." In the days that followed, he excoriated liberal critics of the administration as "nihilists" and traitors. Sounding disquietingly like Joe McCarthy, he warned that "the decadent left in its enclaves along the coasts is not dead—and may well mount what amounts to a fifth column." He denounced Susan Sontag

as "contemptible" and "a pretentious buffoon." He called on America to set a heroic example to the world: "We must show [other countries] as we have never shown them before that a deep humanity and an unremitting rage are not incompatible." On September 16, he appeared to be on his way to the nearest army recruitment center when, having invoked Roosevelt and Churchill, he wrote, "the torch they raised is now passed to us. What a privilege. What an opportunity—especially for my generation and those younger."

For more than two years, Sullivan relentlessly shilled for Bush and for the war on terror, including its "central front" in Iraq. It wasn't until the early months of 2004 that he broke with the "shrewd," "quiet," "underestimated" figure of the President, first over Bush's endorsement of a constitutional ban on gay marriage, then in moral repugnance at the evidence of government-condoned torture at Abu Ghraib. In October 2004, he "endorsed"—as he rather grandly put it, as if he were an editorial board—John Kerry as "the lesser of two risks." Since then he has attacked the administration with all the vehemence he formerly lavished on its detractors. Nowadays, on Sullivan's blog, Rumsfeld is labeled a "war criminal," Bush a "boneless wonder."

In *The Conservative Soul*, he attributes his change of heart to a belated return to rigorous Oakshottian skepticism, and as he expounds Oakeshott, gracefully and in satisfying detail, one is almost won over. Certainly Oakeshott's strictures on the dangers of overweening government power, harnessed to Rationalist dreams and visions, apply very well to the high-handed, high-spending near tyranny of the Bush administration before the midterm elections checked its progress, and Sullivan deserves thanks for bringing Oakeshott into the argument.

But his journalism belies his vaunted skepticism. There is in Sullivan's makeup a most un-Oakshottian quickness to take passionate sides, a schoolboy tendency to hero-worship (Thatcher...Reagan...Oakeshott...Bush...and now it seems he may be warming up fast to Barack Obama), and an Oxford debater's ready access to the rhetoric

of condescending scorn. Where Oakeshott stood self-consciously aloof from practical politics, Sullivan splashes excitedly about in them like a dog in a mud puddle, snarling ferociously at any other dog who challenges his position *du jour*. He's less a skeptic than a mercurial, and somewhat flirtatious, born believer.

So it is—unsurprisingly—on matters of religion that he's at his most persuasive. The book is grounded in Sullivan's tenacious Catholicism, and, as a staunch atheist, I'm impressed by his ability to write plainly, unmawkishly, even movingly, of the intermittent presence of Jesus Christ in his life. He reveres the antiquity of his church, loves the mystery and beauty of its rituals, cherishes the play of nuance and paradox in its theology, but is engaged in a running battle with the present occupant of the Episcopal Palace in Vatican City, Benedict XVI, over the issues of abortion, homosexuality, and, crucially, the role of individual conscience. His Catholicism is so personal and selective that it amounts almost to a kind of Protestantism, specifically Anglo-Catholicism, or High Anglicanism, in its affectionate retention of the forms of the old church while rejecting its authority.

Once upon a time, very long ago, Sir David Frost was capable of being funny. In 1964 or thereabouts, when Sullivan was barely out of diapers, Frost fronted a spoof commercial for the Church of England on the television show *That Was the Week That Was*. Arriving at the punch line, his face a triumphant car-salesman's leer, Frost nasally intoned: "And if you *want* transubstantiation, you can *have* transubstantiation, and if you *don't* want transubstantiation, you needn't *have* transubstantiation." Something of this accommodating spirit informs Sullivan's religion: what he wants, he takes, and what he doesn't want, he doesn't have. He emphatically does not want to submit to the rulings of the man he calls "the fundamentalist pope," whom he effectively excommunicates from his version of the true church. His point is that his beliefs, founded as they are on personal conscience, personal interpretation, shades of meaning, and a neces-

sary embrace of contradictions, are entirely compatible with prag-matic, Oakeshott-style conservatism, while "fundamentalist" beliefs, Catholic or evangelical, are inimical to liberal democracy. It's an argument worth following, even as one notes the amount of special pleading that goes into its construction.

Sullivan's own church, painted in many hues and richly furnished with childhood memories, is seen warmly, from within; those of the American evangelicals are regarded coldly, from without, as when he betrays frank aesthetic distaste for the vulgarity of their architecture —"mega-churches that look and feel like shopping malls and football stadiums." Every age gets the ecclesiastical architecture that its social and political concerns warrant, and it's worth remembering that the great churches of pre-Reformation Europe, which Sullivan loves, look and feel like towered and battlemented military fortresses. Then, churches were built like castles, to intimidate; now, like shopping centers and sports arenas, they take entertainment rather than war as their model, which some might construe as a humanitarian advance of sorts.

Yet Sullivan's alienated eye allows him to probe fundamentalist Christian theology with impressive clarity. Moving among the born-againers like an anthropologist among Yanomami Indians, he breaks their faith down to a nicely lucid series of propositions.

"For the fundamentalist," he writes,

... there is one moment of real conscience, the moment when he makes the decision to conform his mind and will to an external authority. After that, his sole task is obedience, or, at best, being the best student in a class where there is only one set of right answers, prescribed beforehand (and you're allowed, in fact compelled, to see the answers in advance).

These answers all relate to eschatology, to the foreordained apoca-lypse of the "End Times" and the "Rapture," the ultimate event when

living Christians will simultaneously go to Heaven to be with Jesus. To such believers, the course of future history is mapped out in the Bible like a one-way escalator to Doomsday and salvation. (It should perhaps be said that a preoccupation with the fulfillment of ancient prophecies—"that which is written"—is embedded in both the Old and New Testaments, and shapes the thinking of all Christians, not just fundamentalists.) So the millennialist view of the world comes into violent collision with that of Oakeshott, for whom the future was, by definition, incalculable and unknowable. Ironically, Oakeshott would surely have seen the Christian right as Rationalists of the first order.

"Rationalist politics...are the politics of the book," wrote Oakeshott, and Sullivan borrows the phrase to climax a passage on the conflict between his kind of conservatism and the *Weltanschauung* of the fundamentalists:

> For the born-again, there is the life before one is saved and there is the life thereafter. Every fundamentalist life pivots around this bright line. For the conservative, there is merely life—life as a continuing narrative, both personal and communal, a narrative that, like a conversation, has no pre-ordained end and no ultimate truth but the one we give to it. If conservatism is about preserving one's own past, fundamentalism is about erasing it and starting afresh. If conservatism is about the acceptance of imperfection, fundamentalism is about the necessity of perfection now and forever. If conservatism begins with the premise of human error, fundamentalism rests on the fact of divine truth. If conservatism is about the permanence of human nature, fundamentalism looks forward to an apocalypse in which all human nature will be remade by the will of a terrifying and omnipotent God. If conservatism believes in pragmatism and context to determine political choices, fundamentalism relies always on a book. Or rather the Book....

Reading this, a cardinal from Sullivan's church might well sniff heresy ("life...has...no ultimate truth but the one we give to it" sounds particularly dodgy), but it's an eloquent dissection of the underlying rifts in the marriage of convenience between the old right and the religious right—a couple with so little in common at heart that they must lay awake at night in their shared Republican bed, each dreaming of divorce from the other.

In October 2001, Sullivan published an essay in *The New York Times Magazine*, titled "This Is a Religious War." The essay, boldly for those days, likened Jerry Falwell and his fellow American theocrats to Osama bin Laden and the Wahhabist strain of Islam for their shared fear of pluralism, their intolerance born of insecurity, their "blind recourse to texts embraced as literal truth," and their attempt to fuse religious and political authority. That argument is broadened in *The Conservative Soul*, where George W. Bush's narrow religious certitude mirrors the by-the-book certitude of bin Laden and his followers:

> It was...impossible not to see, even in the beginning, the incipient dangers of a fundamentalist mind-set grappling with a huge, complex, and terrifying problem: Islamic fundamentalist terrorism. The absolutism of one almost inescapably triggered the absolutism of the other. 9/11 became, for the president, his second "born-again" moment. Just as a born-again Christian fixates upon a moment on which his entire life now pivots, the born-again presidency redefined itself entirely in terms of an absolute commitment to fighting an abstract enemy, easily conflated into a single entity, readily accessible to the fundamentalist psyche: evil.

That's well said—though if it was really "impossible not to see, even in the beginning," the dangers of the face-off between "Christianists" and Islamists, I'm at a loss to explain why Sullivan so unreservedly signed up for the President's crusade.

As a homosexual, he brings warm personal indignation to bear on the tyranny of "natural law" as it is expounded by conservative Christians such as Robert P. George, the Catholic professor of jurisprudence at Princeton and adviser on bioethics to the Bush administration, who argue that, in Sullivan's words, "human beings have a common, fundamental nature by which they should and must be judged. That nature is given by the Creator and is the arbiter of how we are supposed to live our lives." If our sexuality has a single, divinely ordained purpose, that of procreation, then clearly Sullivan's own sex life has been one long transgression against natural law, and he mounts a sturdy argument in defense of the wide diversity of human sexual experience, practices, and meanings, which makes the natural law theorists sound as dogmatic and disdainful of the empirical evidence as young-earth creationists. He then lucidly extends the same argument to counter the absolutist zealotry of the zygote's-right-to-life brigade, and of the life-at-any-cost-by-whatever-technological-means doctrine to which Tom DeLay and Bill Frist adhered in the Terry Schiavo case.

Sullivan swashbuckles his way through these issues with what seems to me an enviable command of both the relevant science and the relevant theology. When he suggests that if Bush's "theoconservative" spiritual advisers were to have their way, the United States under the present administration would darkly resemble Spain under the Inquisition, England under the Puritan dictatorship of Cromwell, or Afghanistan under the Taliban, he manages to make such comparisons carry a good deal more weight than that of mere rhetorical flourishes.

Montaigne, the third person of Sullivan's trinity, is held up as the shining example of wisdom rooted in humility, curiosity, and wonder. Like Oakeshott, Montaigne saw the circumscribed littleness of human knowledge—the future unforecastable, the present and past imperfectly, myopically perceived. His motto *"Que sais-je?"* might well

have stood as the epigraph to Oakeshott's *Rationalism in Politics*. Sullivan quotes from *The Apology for Raymond Sebond*:

> Since a wise man can be mistaken, and a hundred men, and many nations, yes, and human nature is mistaken for many centuries about this or that, what assurance have we that sometimes it stops being mistaken, and in this century it is not making a mistake?

Later on, Sullivan slangily adapts Montaigne for his own purposes:

> A conservative is defined primarily by his profound grasp of the limits of human understanding. He knows we are always screwing things up; he knows that an idea that seems inspired one day may seem like the dumbest thing on earth a year later.

This may explain Sullivan's painful about-face on the liberal-imperialist conquest of Iraq, but hardly excuses it. It is a self-serving conceit to claim, as he does, that in the days leading up to the invasion, all decent people (excluding the aforementioned nihilists and traitors) were in the same boat, equally misled by what later proved to be defective intelligence on Saddam's weapons of mass destruction:

> I can see the comedy and tragedy of an entire debate almost all of which was premised on what turned out to be a falsehood.... This falsehood was taken as fact by every major intelligence agency and by both supporters and opponents of a war to depose Saddam. We were all wrong.

No we weren't. Many of us at the time preferred to trust the skeptical conservatism of Hans Blix, who had inspected five hundred Iraqi sites by March 2003 and asked for more time, rather than Colin Powell's

"These are not assertions...[but] facts and conclusions based on solid intelligence." We were roundly jeered at by Sullivan for doing so. Montaigne's remarks on the infinite depth of human fallibility were not meant as a license to embrace the one-day inspiration only to reject it as "the dumbest thing on earth" when it turns out badly.

Here, as elsewhere, Sullivan is an opportunist in argument, and sometimes an unscrupulous one. (Shades of the Oxford Union again.) Summoning Thomas Jefferson to prove a point on page 48, he writes, "He did not consider himself a 'secular humanist.' He was a believing Christian." Requiring Jefferson to make another point on page 131, he quotes him: "The day will come when the mystical generation of Jesus, by the Supreme Being as his father, in the womb of a virgin, will be classified with the fable of the generation of Minerva in the brain of Jupiter." Petty consistency is not a hobgoblin that troubles Andrew Sullivan's mind, and he likes to chalk up his inconsistency to his conservatism, because it is a hallmark of the pragmatic conservative to know himself to be frequently mistaken.

Yet in its exposure of the contradictions entailed in being Andrew Sullivan, *The Conservative Soul* rather brilliantly exposes the contradictions of the Republican Party as it is today. If two randomly selected voters who supported Bush in 2000 and 2004 were to be sat in a room and asked to unpack the contents of their heads, each would likely be appalled by the entrenched beliefs of the other. The worldviews of the Christian fundamentalist, the project-driven neoconservative theorist, and the small-government free-marketeer are, as Sullivan shows, dramatically incompatible on both religious and philosophical grounds. Clever as it was of Karl Rove to patch together his grand electoral alliance of radically unlike minds, the arrangement has always had in it the potential for schismatic pandemonium and, since last year's midterms, we've been seeing the stirrings of sectarian warfare in Congress and elsewhere.

As to the question raised in his subtitle—how to "get back" the

soul of conservatism—Sullivan predictably urges his readers to return to Oakeshott's exceptionally modest vision of the scope and power of politics and government. But if his advice were to be followed, a Republican Party in possession of its restored soul would equally alienate the followers of Jerry Falwell and those of Bill Kristol, which, though it may be the stuff of liberal daydreams, is hardly likely to appeal to party strategists. What is so timely about Sullivan's book, and why it should be read closely by liberals as well as conservatives, is its embedded firsthand report on the widening ideological cracks in the house that Rove built—a building that Rove used to boast was permanent and impregnable, and that Sullivan now makes look like a tottering fixer-upper.

—March 15, 2007

POSTSCRIPT

Updating this piece in the heat of a primary season (so far no caucuses have met and no levers have been pulled) is like sending a postcard home that will show up in the mail long after you've arrived yourself—a curled and yellowing souvenir of time past, worth having only because it measures the distance traveled between then and now.

While the Democratic candidates for the presidency are currently trying to balloon small differences of style and biography into major ones of policy, the Republicans appear bent on exposing every rift in the coalition that propelled them to power in 2000 and 2004. Mitt Romney—at the moment sidetracked on the issue of his Mormonism—is the candidate for free-market economics and limited government, and has the endorsement of the *National Review*. Mike Huckabee, rising fast in the polls, is the "Christian Leader," as one of his Iowa ads put it in an unsubtle jibe at Romney's religion, and the prime candidate for the biblical fundamentalists (he's been endorsed

by Jerry Falwell Jr. and Tim LaHaye, author of the "Left Behind" series of novels about the end-times.) Rudolph Giuliani, running on memories of September 11 and emphasizing national security and defense, has enlisted as his chief foreign policy advisers two figures on the neocon far right, Daniel Pipes and Norman "World War IV" Podhoretz, whose views on the Middle East are more vengefully hawkish than those of, say, Paul Wolfowitz, Richard Perle, Douglas Feith, or Vice-President Cheney. John McCain, once seen as the prickly conscience of the mainstream Republican Party and the likely nominee, today is struggling, even in New Hampshire, where he won comfortably in the 2000 primary and has the important endorsement of the old-school-conservative *Union-Leader*. Further toward the fringe of the field, Ron Paul is leading a significant splinter movement for his brand of radical libertarianism.

What divides these five candidates is not ultimately reconcilable shades of emphasis and priority of the kind that divide the Democrats (and divided George W. Bush, John McCain, and Steve Forbes in the 2000 primaries) so much as brute contradictions of worldview. Intellectually and theologically, they're irreconcilable, and their followers belong to different political tribes. Suppose, for instance, that Giuliani, who has been the national front-runner though he's falling in the polls in all the early primary states, eventually wins the nomination: Will Huckabee's substantial flock of monogamous, pro-life, anti-gay, creationist supporters transfer their votes to him? Will any of the losing candidates endorse the party's nominee?

In light of all this, it seems to me that Andrew Sullivan's *The Conservative Soul* has grown steadily more relevant since its publication in the fall of 2006, and is unignorable now. The "Christianists" (Sullivan's term), who were originally intended by Karl Rove to be little more than ballot-fodder in the outer suburbs and the countryside— grassroots social conservatives who, if only they could be driven to the polling booth, would ensure a permanent majority for the Repub-

licans—have risen to dominate the party rhetoric to a degree that Rove can hardly have anticipated. Between their agenda and McCain's or Giuliani's lies a gulf that, to an outsider, looks perfectly unbridgeable. Of course the winning candidate will try to bridge it, but the "concessions" he will have to make will look like acts of rank apostasy to many, if not most, of the people who voted for him first time around.

As for Sullivan himself, early in 2007 I wrote that he appeared to be fast warming up to Barack Obama as the latest object of his political hero-worship. That affair has blossomed. In a stream of articles and blog postings, he has proclaimed Obama to be the last best hope of democracy in the West. But not long ago he was saying much the same thing about George W. Bush, and in the eventful hiatus between my typing these words and their appearing in print, Sullivan's loyalties, like those of Republican primary voters, may well have wandered down entirely unexpected paths.

—December 14, 2007

# 7

## IDEAS FOR DEMOCRATS?

### Frank Rich

IT IS NOT easy to be a professional Democrat in 2006. Out of power for six years and widely damned as out of intellectual steam, the party is regarded in nearly every political precinct and publication as a chronic invalid, doomed to obsolescence even though nearly all the stars are in alignment for a national rejection of all things Bush. When others aren't kicking the Democrats, they are more than happy to kick themselves. The former Clinton hands Rahm Emanuel, now a hard-charging Democratic congressman from Illinois, and Bruce Reed, the president of the centrist Democratic Leadership Council, set the defensive tone of their election-year policy manifesto, *The Plan: Big Ideas for America*,[1] by quoting the Beckett-inflected soliloquy of Ross Perot's ticket mate, Admiral James Stockdale, from the vice-presidential debate of 1992: "Who am I? Why am I here?" These days the Democrats would seem to have fewer answers to such existential questions than the sadly disoriented Stockdale did.

Since John Kerry's defeat in 2004, pundits, Democratic politicians, consultants, bloggers from the "Netroots," and outright quacks have been eager to fill that vacuum, offering often self-contradictory remedies for the party's ailments. First came the religious cure: in desperate

---

1. Public Affairs, 2006.

overreaction to a loaded exit poll suggesting that the Democrats' 2004 showing might in part be due to a "moral values" deficit, party leaders sought out the liberal evangelical author Jim Wallis to learn how they might better make a public fetish of their faith.

Soon to follow was the marketing craze: George Lakoff, the Berkeley linguist and author of *Don't Think of an Elephant!*, advised some of those same leaders on how to "frame" issues so that they, like the Republicans, might popularize hard-to-sell initiatives with their own versions of insidious circumlocutions such as "death tax" and "compassionate conservatism." Other nostrums have included calls for banning pollsters and consultants that package candidates in focus-group-tested platitudes[2] (a capital idea but so far a nonstarter) and a return to talking about class issues[3] (so far taking the tone-deaf form of Wal-Mart bashing, the rare cause embraced by both Joe Lieberman and Ned Lamont).

If all else fails, there's the default position of Clintonism, with or without Hillary Clinton, the putative 2008 presidential front-runner. A widespread fantasy has it that the freshman Illinois Senator Barack Obama, everyone's favorite un-Hillary, might yet be persuaded to throw off caution and run for president while he's still hot rather than waiting until he's "ready." Or perhaps he could serve his apprenticeship on a ticket headed by the new, Hollywood-burnished, and, to many, improved Al Gore.

But whatever the merits of any of these miracle elixirs, the party, no more than Senator Clinton and other potential presidential candidates, still cannot escape the most troubling of the questions that confront it, the question that gets to the heart of "Who am I? Why am I here?" That question, posed by Gary Hart in his own election-year manifesto, *The Courage of Our Convictions*, is this:

---

2. See Joe Klein, *Politics Lost: How American Democracy Was Trivialized by People Who Think You're Stupid* (Doubleday, 2006).

3. See Thomas Frank, "Rendezvous with Oblivion," *The New York Times*, September 1, 2006.

What brought the great Democratic Party, the majority party for much of the twentieth century—the party of Woodrow Wilson and Franklin Delano Roosevelt, the party of Harry Truman, John F. Kennedy, and Lyndon Johnson, the party that successfully led the nation through two world wars and much of the Cold War, the party of the New Deal and the Great Society, the party of great figures and instinctive visionaries, the political home of most of the grand thinking of the twentieth century, the party of civil rights and gender equality, the party that rescued America from the Great Depression, the party of the blue-collar working class and desperate Dust Bowl farmers, the party that provided the ladder of opportunity for generations of immigrants, the party of virtually all progressive movements for a century— what caused that great and historic political institution to cave in so quickly and so willingly to the most questionable military adventure since the invasion of the Philippines a century before?[4]

Neither holding public office nor planning to seek it, Hart has no qualms about addressing forthrightly the non-Republican elephant in the Democrats' room. And the Washington Democrats will have to address it forthrightly too; the war and its aftershocks are not going away. In the campaign years of 2002 and 2004, the party hoped to finesse Iraq by either trying to change the subject to the economy or muddying the issue. Kerry, most memorably, was for the funding of the war before he was against it. Such indirection is untenable now; most polls show that Iraq is the most pressing issue to Americans, a drag on the nation's sense of well-being (as much as 70 percent of the country feels it is on the wrong track) and a spreading threat not just to George W. Bush but also to Congress (which has a lower approval rating than the President does). Left unresolved, Hart's question will

---

4. *The Courage of Our Convictions: A Manifesto for Democrats* (Times Books, 2006).

continue to haunt the party, especially when it must field a national ticket in 2008. The Democrats are unlikely to be persuasive or coherent about national security or foreign policy—or perhaps to be listened to about much else—until they confront their own cave-in to Bush in his rush to war.

There could probably be no more representative illustration of this predicament than Peter Beinart's *The Good Fight*.[5] To his credit, Beinart is attempting to answer Hart's question. As the former editor of *The New Republic* (he has since left that post to become a columnist for the magazine), he was a combative, at times shrill, voice of liberal hawkishness before the war. He has since, like many (nearly all) in his camp, had a change of heart. "I supported the war because I considered it the only remaining way to prevent Saddam Hussein from obtaining a nuclear bomb," he writes in his introduction.

> I also believed it could produce a decent, pluralistic Iraqi regime, which might help open a democratic third way in the Middle East between secular autocrats and their theocratic opponents —a third way that offered the best long-term hope for protecting the United States.

Since there were no aspirations for building such a regime in the Bush White House—Donald Rumsfeld had reaffirmed the administration's long-standing opposition to nation-building in a major speech a month prior to the invasion[6]—this rationalization, also a commonplace among neoconservatives, was wishful armchair punditry at its most fatuous. In any event Beinart now says that he was wrong

---

5. *The Good Fight: Why Liberals—and Only Liberals—Can Win the War on Terror and Make America Great Again* (HarperCollins, 2006).

6. Rumsfeld's speech, "Beyond Nation Building," was delivered at the Intrepid Sea-Air-Space Museum in New York on February 14, 2003. A complete text can be found at www.defenselink .mil/speeches/2003/sp20030214secdef0023.html.

on both counts and on the facts. "But even more important than the facts," he adds, he was wrong on theory. "I was too quick to give up on containment, too quick to think time was on Saddam's side."

His flat-out admission of being "wrong" is refreshing as well as anomalous among former Iraq war enablers. Having bitten that bullet, Beinart, not unlike the Democratic Party, wants to move on. This is not as easy as he might wish. As with the other election-year blueprints for a Democratic future, Beinart bills *The Good Fight* as prescriptive. His subtitle is *Why Liberals—and Only Liberals—Can Win the War on Terror and Make America Great Again*. But for a book that aspires to deal with the future, it is more often than not mired in the past. Much of *The Good Fight* is a good student's rather pedantic recapitulation of cold war history ("The term *totalitarianism* originated in fascist Italy..."), as Beinart sifts through the Truman era and its New Frontier–Vietnam aftermath to arrive at a template for a liberal foreign policy that is both muscular in its opposition to real security threats and circumspect in its acknowledgment of American fallibility and the necessity of multilateral alliances.

Yet the other, far more recent past that shadows his argument is the capitulation of liberals like himself to the Bush Iraq project. This capitulation was far from universal; a majority of Democrats in the House voted against the authorization of the Iraq war, and so did twenty-one Democrats in the Senate. But those who did speed the rush to war included the party's national standard-bearers (John Edwards as well as Kerry) and legislative leaders like the now departed Tom Daschle and Dick Gephardt. For them and, as we see, for Beinart and the many writers like him, this original sin is not so easily exorcised.

"It is a grim irony that this book's central argument is one I myself ignored when it was needed most," Beinart writes. That argument, as he sees it, is "that the morality of American power relies on the limits to American power." But a grimmer irony, perhaps, is that the mea

culpa that opens *The Good Fight* is mitigated by Beinart's persistence in misrepresenting some of the history that preceded the American invasion. He still can be wrong on the facts. In revisiting the dubious arguments he so credulously swallowed before the war, Beinart writes:

> It is impossible to know for sure what would have happened if the inspections had continued into the spring and summer of 2003. But most likely, the inspectors would have grown increasingly certain that Saddam had no nuclear program, and then, at some point Saddam would have kicked them out. Sooner or later, in other words, the United States would have needed a new containment strategy.

Such a new containment effort, Beinart adds, "could certainly have failed."

It is impossible to know for sure what would have happened if inspections had continued, but Beinart's "most likely" scenario wasn't likely at all. When Hans Blix, the chief United Nations weapons inspector, publicly briefed the Security Council on March 7, 2003—twelve days before the American invasion began—he could not have been more explicit about the state of play. "No evidence of proscribed activities have so far been found," Blix said. The Iraqi regime was abandoning conditions it had previously tried to impose on "the exercise of any of our inspection rights." To complete the job, Blix concluded,

> would not take years, nor weeks, but months. Neither governments nor inspectors would want disarmament inspection to go on forever. However, it must be remembered that in accordance with the governing resolutions, a sustained inspection and monitoring system is to remain in place after verified disarmament

to give confidence and to strike an alarm, if signs were seen of the revival of any proscribed weapons programmes.[7]

In other words, after a circumscribed period of months, not years, inspections would have verified the truth: Saddam was bluffing and his WMDs had been almost entirely destroyed in 1991. Containment, which enjoyed the international support that a projected American invasion did not, was working. Had Saddam fulfilled Beinart's hypothesis and tried to kick the inspectors out in the ensuing months, he would have been explicitly violating the governing resolutions' requirement for sustained inspection and monitoring. Thus he would have handed the United States and its allies an unimpeachable, slam-dunk casus belli to go to war. (And that war, which might well have earned the same international support as the weapons' inspections, would not have been the hasty, improvised fiasco that the Bush administration concocted.)

But that's not a likely scenario either. The most likely scenario would have been, as Blix would say in 2005, "continued containment of Iraq rather than war," enforced by continued international inspection of Saddam's weapons capabilities. "It would have carried the modest cost of some $80 million/year and required only 200–300 UN staff. Saddam would have remained—perhaps like a Castro or a Khaddaffi."[8] That this scenario was prevented from unfolding was wholly due to the White House's determination to fix the facts and intelligence around its determination to go to war and, to a lesser extent, to the intellectual and political cover this rash policy received from determined cheerleaders like Beinart.

---

7. Hans Blix, "Briefing of the Security Council, 7 March 2003: Oral introduction of the 12th quarterly report of UNMOVIC." See Hans Blix, *Disarming Iraq* (Pantheon, 2004), p. 210, and also UN resolutions 687 (1991) and 1284 (1999). Resolution 1441 (2002) left the earlier provisions for a monitoring system intact.

8. Blix, "Controlling Weapons of Mass Destruction—Lessons of Iraq," The Margolis Lecture, May 5, 2005, UCI's Center for Global Peace and Conflict Studies, Irvine, California.

In all his pages about the war fever that he helped gin up, Beinart still finds it hard to concede in plain language the simple facts of the matter, which are summarized without dependent clauses by Senator Edward Kennedy in his own election-year book-length campaign document, *America Back on Track*: "If America had allowed the UN inspections to be continued, war could have been avoided. We were never given a convincing reason by the administration to remove the inspectors and launch the invasion."[9] Beinart's concession that he was "wrong" on the facts and the theory is welcome, but his explanation for this failure is at best disingenuous: "Worst-case logic became a filter, preventing war supporters like myself from seeing the evidence mounting around us."

Standing on this shaky platform, he offers himself as a guide to the future. Taking as a departure point the 1947 meeting at the Willard Hotel where the Americans for Democratic Action purged Henry Wallace and Communist fellow travelers from their ranks, Beinart posits a reborn foreign policy in the tradition of cold war anti-totalitarian liberalism. Democrats must retrieve the mantle of tough-minded containment from the era of Truman, Marshall, and Kennan. They must reawaken to the hardheaded liberal realism of Arthur Schlesinger Jr. and Reinhold Niebuhr, battling jihadist terrorism without Bush's cowboy recklessness and with self-restraint: "In the liberal vision, national greatness is not inherited and it is not declared; it is earned." Unlike Bush's war on terror, this policy will be tethered to a belief in human rights. It will win hearts and minds with a new Marshall Plan. Its hallmarks will include collaborating both with allies and with international bodies—i.e., with the likes of Hans Blix.

Much of this is commendable, picking up where second-term Clinton foreign policy, as tardily practiced in the Balkans, left off. Some of it is based on dubious, if not simplistic, analogies: Is decentralized

---

9. Viking, 2006.

Islamic terrorism, with fundamentalist religion at its angry core, interchangeable with secular totalitarianism, whether Stalin's or Saddam's, and can it really be fought by schematically analogous means?[10] Some of Beinart's program is simply wishful thinking. If Truman and Marshall came back from the dead, they could not sell a Marshall Plan to the isolationist and xenophobic America that the Iraq war has left in its wake, not just among some Democrats (as Beinart bemoans) but, in an even more virulent form, among the Republican base.[11] The Marshall Plan we theoretically brought to Iraq, a $22 billion farrago of waste and corruption, will serve as a poster child against foreign aid in congressional races for years.

But for the most part Beinart's prescription is already conventional wisdom in much of the Democratic Party: as a piece of rhetoric, *The Good Fight* seems to be a Rube Goldberg contraption laboring hard to fling open an already open door. Emanuel and Reed, for instance, call for "a muscular, progressive strategy to use all the tools of American power to make America safe in a dangerous world" and for enlisting "our allies in a common mission against the conditions" that breed terrorism. They specifically endorse *The Good Fight* and the nearly identical argument for "progressive internationalism" set out earlier by Will Marshall of the Progressive Policy Institute.[12] Indeed,

---

10. For a more complex view than Beinart's of Sayyid Qutb, the philosophical godfather of modern jihadism, see Lawrence Wright, *The Looming Tower: Al-Qaeda and the Road to 9/11* (Knopf, 2006), reviewed by Robert Worth in *The New York Review*, October 19, 2006. For instance: "The distinctions between capitalism and Marxism, Christianity and Judaism, fascism and democracy were insignificant by comparison with the single great divide in Qutb's mind: Islam and the East on the one side, and the Christian West on the other." Qutb's progeny are not so easily interchanged with America's cold war adversaries, though Beinart labors to present them as such.

11. See Patrick J. Buchanan, *State of Emergency: The Third World Invasion and Conquest of America* (Thomas Dunne Books, 2006).

12. See, for instance, Will Marshall, "Closing the National Security Gap," *Blueprint*, July 25, 2004.

Beinart's position, an aggressive pursuit of terrorists joined with multilateralism and fidelity to democratic ideals, often sounds like the one that Kerry tried to articulate, none too clearly, during the 2004 campaign. In *The Plan*, Emanuel and Reed up the ante by calling for an additional 100,000 troops for the Army and an unspecified number of additions to the US Special Forces and the Marines. (They do not say whether they should be added before or after we leave Iraq.)

What undermines the sounder policy prescriptions in *The Good Fight* is its underlying animus—an animus that is all too much in keeping with the mindset that led Beinart and others like him to embrace the Iraq war with few questions and much self-righteous arrogance in 2002 and early 2003. However many quarrels he has with the Bush administration, Beinart is still hoping to prove that those who did not get it wrong were somehow wrong anyway—or at least more wrong than he was, and more frivolous. This leads him to echo the Bush White House, as he attempts to conflate the serious pre-invasion opponents of the Iraq war with a mindless, cut-and-run mob of peaceniks who don't understand the threats to national security posed by Islamic radicalism, who opposed war in Afghanistan and who now can't be trusted to protect America because they're too busy hating Bush to take on terrorists. He warns darkly that this crowd could yet hijack the Democratic Party with apocalyptic results:

> For too many liberals today, George W. Bush's war on terror is the only one they can imagine.... If today's liberals cannot rouse as much passion for fighting a movement that flings acid at unveiled women as they do for taking back the Senate in 2006, they have strayed far from liberalism's best traditions. And if they believe it is only George W. Bush who threatens America's freedoms, they should ponder what will happen if the United States is hit with a nuclear or contagious biological attack. No

matter who is president, Republican or Democrat, the reaction will make John Ashcroft look like the head of the ACLU.

"Many liberals?" How many? Such overstatement, bordering on hysteria and laced with unearned condescension, is a common tic among liberal pundits who supported the war in Iraq and now regret it. This impulse came out in force after the victory of Ned Lamont over Joe Lieberman in the Democratic senatorial primary in Connecticut. Writing in *Slate*, for instance, Jacob Weisberg argued that Lamont's victory over Lieberman "spells Democratic disaster" because it will lead the party to "re-enact a version of the Vietnam-era drama that helped them lose five out of six presidential elections between 1968 and the end of the Cold War." Though conceding (in a marvelously revealing phrase) that "Lieberman's opponents are not entirely wrong about the war," Weisberg lamented that too many of those opponents "appear not to take the wider, global battle against Islamic fanaticism seriously."[13]

"Appear," of course, is as elastic a formulation as Beinart's "many liberals." Appear where? Usually on blogs, especially (in Beinart's book) those at MoveOn Peace (since subsumed into Moveon.org), whose most naive post–September 11 pacifists he quotes with relish. Such bloggers certainly represent a constituency within the Democratic Party (or those that believe in the two-party system do). But there's no evidence to support the liberal hawks' fear that peaceniks who minimize the threat of Islamic fanaticism amount to a sizable contingent anywhere in America, including among Democrats. If this is a movement, it is one with no plausible national candidate or even statewide candidate (including Lamont, who is against the Iraq war but not against Beinart's good fight against Islamic terrorists). Its most popular leader by far is Michael Moore, whose most risible

---

13. "Dead with Ned: Why Lamont's Victory Spells Democratic Disaster," *Slate*, August 9, 2006.

leftist preachments are examined from as far back as 1986 in *The Good Fight*. Implicitly serving as the boogeyman heir both to Henry Wallace and his fellow travelers and to New Left radicals who greased the skids for the debacle of the McGovern campaign, the boorish filmmaker is Beinart's exemplar of the kind of mindless lefty tempting to lead the Democrats astray.

He's also a straw man. It's hard to argue that Moore, a diva whose shtick is hyperbole and provocation, has fomented any movement that threatens to take over the Democratic Party or even Hollywood. *Fahrenheit 9/11*—seen by less than a third of the audience of leading 2004 hits like *Shrek 2* and *The Passion of the Christ*—did not move election results; it did prompt an outpouring of liberal documentaries, most of which have barely registered at the box office (Gore's *An Inconvenient Truth* being a modest exception). However many reflexive pacifists there may be in Moore's audience, or at Cindy Sheehan rallies, or on blogs, the number of Americans who opposed defeating al-Qaeda and the Taliban after September 11 was a tiny fringe; Bush enjoyed nearly 90 percent–plus support, including for the war in Afghanistan, with good reason.

The tragedy is that when Bush betrayed the country's trust and hijacked a united citizenry for his own ends there were too many liberals who went MIA, whether in Congress or on opinion pages, at a time, as Beinart concedes, when such a principled opposition "was needed most." That opposition could have rallied around the same principles that are espoused in *The Good Fight* without succumbing to Bush propaganda about a war that has done more to harm the battle against terrorism than any blogging pacifist has. It would have been a far better thing for the country if liberal hawks had articulated those principles clearly then without compromising them. Their inability to do so was a systemic intellectual failure that Beinart's book only begins to address. And while it's better late than never to stand up for the credo outlined in *The Good Fight*, what current

Democratic leader does not now endorse the same basic national security catechism as Beinart's, from Howard Dean to Hillary Clinton? The only real debate among Democrats today is over the timetable for the inevitable drawdown of American troops from Iraq, not from the battle against Islamic terrorists. So limited is the power of the leftist activists feared by Beinart that they have been unable to persuade most Democratic candidates in tight election races in the fall of 2006 to support any plan for a precipitous Iraq withdrawal.[14]

Even Gary Hart, who served as McGovern's campaign manager in the ill-fated presidential campaign so central to the cautionary tales in *The Good Fight*, endorses the same foreign policy thinking as Beinart. Hart writes:

> It is imperative now that the Democratic Party restore the Truman principle of international alliance. If for no other reason, the struggle to suppress jihadist terrorism demands it. The center of radical Islamic jihad is not solely in the Middle East, it is in Europe as well.... It will prove impossible for the United States to defend itself against the international jihad without maintaining a close integration of Western intelligence agencies, secret services, and special forces.

The only real difference between Hart's prescriptions and Beinart's is that Hart is not losing sleep that the Democratic Party might be taken over by insurgents and does not make facile analogies between angry Bush-hating bloggers and the far more tumultuous, numerous, and radical New Left brigades of the 1960s.

---

14. See Jim VandeHei and Zachary A. Goldfarb, "Democrats Split Over Timetable for Troops," *The Washington Post*, August 27, 2006. Even Eric Massa, a staunch antiwar candidate supported by MoveOn.org for a congressional seat in western New York State, does not call for an immediate withdrawal from Iraq. See John M. Broder, "What Would the Democrats Do?" *The New York Times*, September 17, 2006.

Beinart's hyperventilating over the threat of a supposedly resurgent left is a reminder of the habits of mind that led him to the mistakes this book wants to apologize for. Once again, worst-case logic has become a filter, preventing him from looking clearly at the evidence. Writing of liberal activists who blog at dailykos.com, he frets that "their idealism, and their outrage, is directed almost exclusively against the right." But that's the point of Daily Kos, which is a blog for letting off steam about partisan Democratic politics. At the equivalent Republican blogs, the outrage is directed almost exclusively against liberals. That the most volatile liberal bloggers rage at Bush more than at bin Laden and that their conservative counterparts rage at Nancy Pelosi more than at Zawahiri has nothing to do with the price of fish, except red herrings.

Once Beinart leaves foreign policy behind in *The Good Fight* to race through a laundry list of domestic policy points, he shows that it's impossible to reinvent the wheel. From old liberal lions like Kennedy and Hart to Democratic Leadership Council centrists like Emanuel and Reed, everyone espouses variations on the same central principles Beinart does, whether they are the "Seven Challenges" specified by Kennedy (a happy middle ground between his brother's eight profiles in courage and Nixon's six crises) or the five big ideas bite-sized enough to "be counted off on one hand" in *The Plan*. With some variations, all endorse universal health care, energy conservation, universal citizen service along the Peace Corps/AmeriCorps model, a reduction in income inequality, a restoration of constitutional protections of rights, and so on. Their renewed case for liberal governance is of a piece with Michael Tomasky's influential essay arguing for a Democratic Party that stands for the core principle of the "common good" rather than a list of discrete planks pandering to every conceivable constituency.[15]

---

15. "Party in Search of a Notion," *The American Prospect*, May 2006.

It is hard to imagine a large public listening intently to any of it as long as their government is enmeshed in a war with little promise of a happy resolution and no known exit strategy. Like Beinart, other Washington Democrats who endorsed the Iraq adventure on the way in are all too glad to talk about the long war against jihadists going forward, but all too cautious about confronting the endgame in Iraq. What the party transparently lacks is not ideas or pundits offering advice, but leaders. Those Democratic politicians who might lead have no intention of doing so until the night of November 7, 2006, after the voters have told them what to think.

—September 21, 2006

### POSTSCRIPT

Such was the low estate of the Bush administration in American public opinion that the Democrats did even better than expected in the midterm elections of 2006, especially in their narrow takeover of the Senate. The most revealing upset came in Virginia, where Jim Webb, a much-decorated Vietnam veteran, fierce Iraq war critic, and former secretary of the navy in the Reagan administration, beat the incumbent Republican senator, George Allen. Many Republican insiders had long envisioned Allen as the party's next presidential standard-bearer. Like George W. Bush, he was an unalloyed conservative with a talent for hiding his hard ideological edges behind a jocular good-old-boy persona. But a campaign incident widely disseminated on the video Web site YouTube, in which Allen addressed an Indian-American campaign worker for Webb with a racial slur ("macaca"), ripped off the mask, cost him his Senate seat and, in all likelihood, his political career.

The once reliably red Virginia was changing faster than either Allen or the national GOP had reckoned. The target of Allen's insult

was a high-achieving college student, the scion of an immigrant family typical of the high-tech industry workers that have been steadily upending the old voting patterns in Washington's northern Virginia suburbs. Yet Allen seemed oblivious. In the YouTube incident, he didn't merely address the student with a crude name but followed up with a nativist-scented insult: "Welcome to America and the real world of Virginia."

That many Republicans ignored the broader implications of this incident—and of the failure of two of the party's most vociferous illegal-immigration demagogues to hold House seats in Arizona—may be crucial to Democratic hopes in 2008, should all else fail. Blithely stumbling on in the months after Election Day 2006, some of the GOP's most vocal political and media figures, including much of its incipient presidential field, escalated their truculent border-panic rhetoric. Winning Hispanic recruits for the party had been a major and often successful project for Bush and Karl Rove, starting in Texas, but as election year dawned, that ambition lay in ruins. The GOP's rampant xenophobia threatened to swing Hispanic votes in the closely fought states of Colorado, Arizona, New Mexico, Nevada, and Florida in 2008. All five had gone for Bush in 2004. Their total electoral votes, fifty-six, dwarf those of, say, Ohio (twenty).

The Democrats' congressional take-over in 2006 did push their leadership to unequivocally embrace an Iraq endgame. But it has not resolved the party's intellectual dilemmas or guaranteed it a lock on 2008. President Bush still benefited from a remarkably unified Republican caucus in Congress and, for the first time in his presidency, brandished the veto pen. Unable to affect White House war policy, the Democratic-led Congress, fairly or not, lost much of the moral high ground on Iraq with voters, giving Republicans an opportunity to blur distinctions between the two parties as the public waited for a coherent exit strategy. And waited impatiently. Though repeated polls at the end of 2007 found that voters recognized the improved security

in Iraq after the "surge," those same surveys found that the majorities calling for a prompt withdrawal and terming the war "a mistake" remained unchanged from the war's most violent nadir. Congress soon found itself with approval ratings as low as and sometimes lower than the President's. The number of Americans who judged their country to be "on the wrong track" remained stuck at 70 percent and higher, views that were soon to be complemented by an economic gloom as thick as any pollsters had seen since the early 1990s.

The Democrats' conflicted history on Iraq haunts the presidential campaign. Unlike John Edwards or pundits like Peter Beinart, Hillary Clinton refused to acknowledge that her support for the 2002 war resolution was a mistake. Instead, her husband disingenuously declared that he, at least, had been against the Iraq war "from the beginning." When that ruse failed, the Clinton campaign tried to muddy Barack Obama's early opposition to the war, a signature element of his presidential candidacy, by claiming (also incorrectly) that he had gone wobbly in the years since. Meanwhile, every Democratic candidate called for the war's quick end (though Clinton had the loosest timetable). Every major Democratic candidate took a muscular stand on foreign policy in general and terrorism in particular rather than emulating the party's supposed mob of MoveOn.org–Netroots peaceniks so hyperbolically caricatured and feared by liberal hawks who had initially supported the Iraq war.

On domestic issues, the most energetic class-conscious populist appeal, made by Edwards, gained at most modest traction in the early going. Clinton and Obama, whatever the fine points of their policy differences, hewed to standard party orthodoxy. Clinton's laundry list of programs recalled her husband's centrism (and triangulation); she seemed to be campaigning for a third Clinton term. Obama's domestic agenda was united by a larger, reconciliatory theme that at times echoed Michael Tomasky's notion of a "common good." But if the early 2008 votes in Iowa and New Hampshire were any

indication, the race for the Democratic nomination was going to be a scramble built less on policy than on a wide variety of factors including race, gender, negative campaigning, and the usual unpredictable events of any political season.

However much the Democrats might finesse differences on Iraq or any other issue in 2008, their best hopes for electoral victory still have less to do with their own ideas than with the sorry state of their opponents. Compared to the increasingly fractious and disheartened conservative coalition, the Democrats could pass for a model of coherence and unity. Compared to the Bush presidency, almost any conceivable Democratic ticket would seem a step up to the vast majority of voters eager to turn the page. The Democrats could yet lose the White House in 2008, especially if the general election becomes a referendum on the Clintons or race, but it would take the party's full powers of self-immolation to do so.

—January 17, 2008

# 8

## THE DEMOCRATS

## *Michael Tomasky*

WHATEVER ELSE HAPPENS on January 20, 2009, the date on which, barring impeachment or tragedy, George W. Bush will finally leave office, the day will mark a rather surprising historical fact. As Mark Halperin and John F. Harris point out in their introduction to *The Way to Win*,[1] it will be the first time since the consecutive administrations of James Madison and James Monroe that "back-to-back presidents both served all eight years of two elected terms." Monroe's term ended in 1825. In every era since, death, scandal, political failure, or some other kind of disruption—notably, a broad political shift that ends one era and begins another—has intruded upon the presidential succession process, until now.

In our own time, why have things been different? We can look at the administrations of Bill Clinton and George W. Bush and locate specific reasons—that Clinton had the economy humming along and thus gave voters no reason to turn him out in 1996, and that Bush responded to September 11 by putting the country on a war footing and built his reelection campaign around making voters afraid to turn him out. We can also chalk it up to the weak competition from Bob Dole and John Kerry, whose races were utterly without focus.

---

1. *The Way to Win: Taking the White House in 2008* (Random House, 2006).

But I suspect there may be a more systemic reason. We entered our current era of polarization in 1992, when a well-funded conservative echo machine worked to destroy Clinton, a project that never let up until the day he left office (the Marc Rich pardon, the White House furniture "scandal"). Once conservatives gained power, they held on to it tenaciously, initiating horrifically radical turns in foreign and domestic policy from which we'll spend years recovering. But for all this ideological volatility, our sharply polarized era has produced comparatively few lasting shifts in voter identification or allegiance. Students of this subject and television commentators tend, understandably, to highlight the changes that show up from election to election. And while there have been fluctuations in the intervening years (occasionally decisive ones, such as in 1994, when the Democratic vote dropped among almost all groups), after the fall 2006 election we are almost back where we were in 1992.

For example, *New York Times* exit poll data[2] covering the period show the following: men voted 52 percent Democratic in 1992, and, after dropping into the mid-40s for a while, were back to 52 percent Democratic again in 2006. Women voted 55 percent Democratic in 1992, and 52 percent Democratic in 2006 (this vote hardly changed, except in 2002, when it went down to 50 percent); whites voted 50 percent Republican in 1992, and 52 percent Republican in 2006 (remember that H. Ross Perot ran as an independent in 1992, thus lowering white Republican votes slightly).[3] One significant difference is in independent voters, among whom Democrats went from 54 percent in 1992 to 59 percent in 2006. But it's too early to call that a trend.

---

2. Data are available at www.nytimes.com/2006/11/08/us/politics/20061108_ELECTION_PORTRAIT_HOUSE.html?ex=1169182800&en=3c67ea3bce8ee5de&ei=5070. My thanks to Ruy Teixeira, a Century Foundation and Center for American Progress fellow and respected exit poll analyst, for helping me locate these and other numbers.

3. There are some exceptions. In 1992, Clinton persuaded 15 percent of Republicans to vote for him. But by 1996, only 8 percent of Republicans voted Democratic—the same percentage as in 2006.

Other periods of American history have brought vast realignments, crisply demarcated in single presidential elections, as when FDR took over from Herbert Hoover. Voting blocs have disappeared and emerged, forcing the parties to reshape themselves. But in our recent history, the two parties, and the kinds of Americans who tend to cluster within them, have fought to a draw—the irresistible force of secular belief in public investment set against the immovable object of faith-based laissez-faireism, each nipping at the other, but no more. In view of the results in 2002 and 2004, Karl Rove used to speak of a "rolling realignment," predicting that today's Republicans would accomplish over three or four elections what the 1932 Democrats and the 1896 Republicans pulled off in one. This was mostly spin, but for a time, it had the look of spin that might just become reality, and a credulous press bought into it. After November 2006, Rove's dream is in ashes. Polarization has yielded a kind of electoral stasis, with both parties and the coalitions within them staying remarkably united and scratching and clawing to hold on to presidential power once they have it.

Four elections is a long time in politics for a grudge match. Something usually gives in the space of fifteen years. Even so potent a force as Reagan conservatism, it may fairly be said, lasted only ten; it took a body blow in the fall of 1990, when George H. W. Bush's administration, in secretive budget negotiations held at Andrews Air Force Base, agreed to tax increases. This broke Bush's "read my lips" pledge from the 1988 convention, infuriating conservatives and taking some of the sizzle out of their movement. If you ask conservatives why Bush lost to Clinton, they will point first not to Clintonian charisma or the case for generational change made by Clinton and Al Gore; they will speak chiefly of what happened at Andrews Air Force Base.[4]

---

4. And sometimes with humor. "Munich, you can kind of make a case for Munich," the conservative activist Grover Norquist once told me jokingly. "But Andrews Air Force Base... never!"

MICHAEL TOMASKY

Today, George W. Bush is weakened, the nation restless to be done with him.[5] In the eyes of many voters Bush has not only discredited himself; he has to some extent discredited conservatism. For the first time in at least a decade, one senses at least the potential for large-scale shifts, for some yet-unknown X-factor to break the logjam. After the 2006 elections, there is reason to think that these shifts will redound to the Democrats' benefit. At the same time, there is danger for Democrats in reading too much into the 2006 vote. As Chuck Schumer notes in *Positively American*,[6] the party's 2006 successes were built more around a negative message about Bush and congressional Republicans than any affirmative case the party made and "were not the sign of a lasting Democratic majority." And while Democrats in Congress have united to pass the handful of uncontroversial planks on which they did run—a higher minimum wage, a college tuition tax credit—the fact is that the party remains split on major foreign and domestic policy questions. This split was if anything intensified by the 2006 results, particularly on the always barbed issues of globalization and trade, on which the party's liberal wing gained momentum with the election of such economic populists as Sherrod Brown of Ohio and Jim Webb of Virginia.

Finally, there are the questions of 2008: Who will be the Democrats' nominee for president, and how will that choice affect the center of gravity? The three leading contenders—Hillary Clinton, John Edwards, and Barack Obama—are making starkly different pitches to voters, based on quite different assumptions about what the party needs to do to break the stalemate. The next year and a half—in which we'll

5. One of the most remarkable poll results I've ever seen: in late January 2007, after the State of the Union address, CNN asked respondents various questions about Bush, and 58 percent said they "wish the Bush presidency was simply over." See www.cnn.com/POLITICS/blogs/politicalticker/2007/01/ bushs-approval-sags-to-record-low-in.html.

6. Senator Chuck Schumer, with Daniel Squadron, *Positively American: Winning Back the Middle-Class Majority One Family at a Time* (Rodale, 2007).

see if the Democrats make a success of their congressional majority and who captures the presidential nomination—will be the most consequential eighteen months the party has faced in some time.

How could the Democrats go about building a lasting majority? Schumer has some definite ideas. Of all the national leaders the Democratic Party has produced in recent years, few are as manically driven as New York's senior senator. He has been a politician his entire adult life—he graduated from Harvard Law School in 1974 and, returning to his old neighborhood off Kings Highway in Brooklyn, he immediately ran for, and won, a seat in New York's state assembly. He moved up to the House of Representatives in 1980. Intellectually liberal in the way of New York City Democrats, instinctively conservative in the manner of his outer-borough bedroom community, and with an unstoppable hunger for press attention, he made a name for himself passing legislation like the Brady Bill on handguns. He toyed with running for governor but in 1997 decided instead to seek the Senate seat held by Al D'Amato. In January 1998, he was a distant third in polls in the Democratic primary behind Geraldine Ferraro and Mark Green; by the time of the September primary, he'd demolished them both. That November, he polished off D'Amato. Some months afterward, Schumer writes in his book, a still-astonished D'Amato offered a two-sentence analysis of their contest that describes both D'Amato's worldview and Schumer's relentlessness: "I couldn't scare you, Chuck. You've got the two biggest ones in the state."

In 2005, Schumer assumed the chairmanship of the Democratic Senatorial Campaign Committee (DSCC), thus taking on the responsibilities of finding plausible Senate candidates and raising the many millions needed to elect them. For most senators, the post is the equivalent of KP duty—a task they grudgingly accept if entreated by the leadership. Most are greatly relieved when their two-year tour of duty ends. Schumer, who calls rich people to put the touch on them with

the same ardor with which he attends upstate county fairs, and who obviously did the job well, has signed up for another term.[7]

Schumer has not so far emerged as an intellectual leader in the party, but anyone with his record of success—New York Republicans didn't bother to muster more than token opposition to him in 2004— is worth listening to when he talks about what his party needs to do. And in fact, Schumer's analysis of historic political and social changes in the book's early chapters is often trenchant. He points to three long-term trends that ate away at New Deal–style liberalism: the success of Democratic governance, which lifted millions into prosperity and "made them forget the role government had played in facilitating that success"; the homogenization of the country, which weakened Democratic appeals to groups of voters based on ethnic or regional identity[8]; and the decreasing appeal, as capitalism succeeded for more and more people who vote, of a politics based on criticism of the status quo and egalitarian economic and social policies. These changes helped grease conservatism's path to power.

But more recent history—specifically, the vast technological changes that have transformed our economic and social life—helps explain conservatism's current difficulties. The Internet, the globalized economy, outsourcing, and the "ability to transfer huge amounts of information quickly and at virtually no cost" have created new social conditions. The conservative insistence that the market will fairly sort out winners and losers is, he writes, inadequate to the times:

> Since the early 1990s, technology has so revolutionized the landscape that the Republican answer of twenty-five years ago

7. Incidentally, the map of Senate elections taking place in 2008 looks potentially quite favorable to Democrats. Republicans must defend twenty-one seats, and Democrats just twelve.

8. The exception here, as Schumer notes, is African-Americans, who because of racism and legal barriers have maintained a stronger group identity than the Irish or Italians.

—strangle the government—no longer works.... As a result, as in 1932 and 1980, the political loyalty of the middle class is once again up for grabs.

Schumer's fixation on the middle class is such that he has even invented a couple, Joe and Eileen Bailey of Massapequa (at one point he goes so far as to refer to them as "actual, albeit imaginary"), who, average in every way, serve as his lodestar. Franklin Roosevelt might have wanted to "clear it with Sidney," in the famous phrase referring to union leader Sidney Hillman's influence with Roosevelt. But Schumer clears everything with Joe and Eileen.[9] The prescriptions he lays out in the book's final twelve chapters—increase reading and math scores, reduce property taxes, reduce illegal immigration while increasing legal immigration, reduce cancer mortality, reduce abortions, cut children's access to Internet pornography; all by 50 percent—are aimed obsessively at them.

Certainly, any political party seeking at least 51 percent of the votes must be attuned to the needs of the middle class, and it would be foolish to belittle the importance of the issues Schumer writes about. But sometimes leaders must lead instead of cater. He allows at one point that "I would not act purely on the basis of what Joe and Eileen wanted." But his "50 percent solutions" give little indication of this. They include nothing about universal health care or global warming or reducing poverty or rebuilding New Orleans or indeed about any larger vision for the country. And it's clear why: these are not safe issues since the Baileys won't find that their self-interest is at stake in any of them. On issues like these, it is up to politicians to encourage in the Baileys of America an awareness and an empathy

---

9. Political reporters have heard Schumer speak of Joe and Eileen for a few years now. In *Positively American*, he fills out the family picture. Their three children are named Megan, Abby, and Pete. In the last two years, Pete has "grown fatter," which has the Baileys fretting about child obesity.

that they would not otherwise have. Or, to take another example, there's Iraq. It seems likely that Schumer's imaginary friends would, like most Americans at the time, have supported the case for war back in October 2002, when the Senate voted to authorize unconditionally the use of force against Iraq. And sure enough, Schumer voted for the war. That was catering to the Baileys, all right. But it was a disgraceful vote, which poorly served his country, his party, and, as I'm sure they'd now agree, his beloved Baileys.

I've dwelled on Schumer's book because he is a very powerful man now. He's part of the Democratic Senate leadership, and he's helped elect six freshman senators who are all to one degree or another in his debt, with more like them on the way. He is at the center of the highest-level Democratic debates about strategy and policy, and we know that the Democrats will listen to him.

What we don't know about the Democrats at this point is whether the party has an interest in summoning Americans to think about the world from a broader perspective than how a given issue affects them directly. If Schumer is right about the present Democratic opportunity, and I suspect he is, then the question arises whether that opportunity is best seized by deciding what average people want and giving it to them, or whether, in addition to that, leaders should aim a bit higher, addressing the larger issues that Schumer ignores. It is one thing to speak to people as consumers and as parents. But is it possible to speak to people as citizens, asking them to participate in something that has a larger national purpose?

This makes many Washington Democrats uneasy—it sounds to them like mushy idealism, and, far worse, like it might require them to get into a debate about raising taxes.[10] But there are small glim-

---

10. For a fascinating analysis of the changing politics of tax cuts, positing that the era of the tax revolt (which started in the late 1970s) is over, see "Read My Lips: Raise Taxes," by Mark Schmitt, *The Washington Monthly*, January/February 2007.

mers. In *The Plan*,[11] Rahm Emanuel, the Chicago congressman who was Schumer's counterpart in the House last fall as chairman of the Democratic Congressional Campaign Committee, and Bruce Reed, the Clinton White House domestic policy adviser who now edits the Democratic Leadership Council magazine *Blueprint*, speak of "a politics of national purpose" and write that "if your leaders aren't challenging you to do your part, they aren't doing theirs." Their most tangible manifestation of this principle is their call for a "universal citizen service" program, under which people between the ages of eighteen and twenty-five would have to enlist for three months of civilian service. This builds on Bill Clinton's Americorps volunteer program but does away with the voluntary part. One can also hear in it a strong echo of Camelot, and indeed Emanuel and Reed consciously invoke John Kennedy's influence. But requiring young people to spend three months in a youth corps at government expense is the low-hanging fruit of civic engagement; it's not exactly the stuff of which realignments are made.

There is much on which Democrats of all persuasions agree. Emanuel and Reed are careful to base *The Plan* mostly on work done by centrist policy intellectuals, but they avoid the contentious questions that separate centrists and liberals, such as the long-running debate about budget balancing versus public investment. Instead, they emphasize policies that Democrats can agree on. They call, among other things, for making broadband access universal, for cutting gasoline consumption in half, and for cracking down on corporate welfare. And Democrats agree that Bush has pursued ruinous policies, and on the need to fight back—an argument made, with numerous examples, by James Carville and Paul Begala in *Take It Back*[12] ("the problem with the Democratic Party is not ideological, it's

---

11. *The Plan: Big Ideas for America* (Public Affairs, 2006).

12. *Take It Back: A Battle Plan for Democratic Victory* (Simon and Schuster, 2006).

anatomical. We lack a backbone"). Their book is self-consciously folksy; the Republicans are "so incompetent they couldn't pour pee out of a boot if you wrote the instructions on the heel." But buried under these apothegms is a surprisingly expert catalog of the issues of the day, with specific instructions on how to "take back" the initiative on issues of tax policy and health care and the abortion debate. For example, the authors recommend that on tax policy, Democrats answer Republican demands for more tax cuts by emphasizing fairness to the middle class and by showing that tax cuts for the rich exacerbate larger economic problems, such as our debt to China and Japan. It may seem obvious, this need to fight back. But for quite some time, most elected Democrats in Washington did not do so, because they feared Bush and Rove. Recall the decision at the party's 2004 convention in Boston to restrict the attacks on Bush from the podium (the Republicans, at their convention, felt no such compunction).

But these developments, and the flush of general unity that has accompanied the Democrats' victory in Congress, shouldn't obscure the deep disagreements that persist within the party. On Capitol Hill, Democrats will likely be able to paper over many of these differences, on economic and especially social issues, which Republicans have used to such advantage in recent years. Since they control the legislative calendar, Democrats will see to it that issues that divide and terrify them, like gay marriage or flag-burning, won't come up for votes. But they can't make them disappear completely, and although Democrats felt relieved that in 2006 there was no replay of 2004, when anti–gay marriage initiatives in eleven states brought religious conservatives to the polls in large numbers, no one can say with confidence that controversies like this have gone away for good. (One fatefully timed decision by a liberal state supreme court legalizing gay marriage, and we're back to 2004.)

Is there a middle ground for Democrats on contentious questions such as this? Carville and Begala see themselves as dispensing tactical

advice to Democratic officials. But David Callahan struggles nobly to find something deeper in *The Moral Center*.[13] A senior fellow at Demos, a public policy center based in New York, Callahan rejects the argument of Thomas Frank in *What's the Matter with Kansas?* that working-class voters have been tricked by right-wingers into voting against their own economic interests. Instead, he asserts, "moral concerns have become bigger issues" than economic concerns for these voters; besides, he writes, "liberals vote their values all the time. No one asks, 'What's the matter with Cambridge?'" (It might have made a good title for his book.) He traveled around the country and talked with many people of the left and the right trying to find common ground on moral issues. As one expects, there isn't very much. Callahan wants liberals to embrace moderates who have conflicting feelings about these questions—the Baileys, you might say—to create a new public morality that is concerned about both poverty and video game violence, both wages and rap lyrics. He wants to soften the jagged edges of the culture wars.

To which Laura Flanders says: nonsense! Flanders, who hosts a show on Air America Radio, surveys in her new book *Blue Grit*[14] the opinions of white men who wrote after the 2004 election that the Democrats should sidestep cultural fights and answers that "culture war by culture war is how American history has advanced." She recalls for example the abolition of slavery, the suffrage movement, and the more recent efforts of gays to gain equal rights. Flanders, too, traveled the country, but it seems unlikely that she and Callahan bumped into each other, because Flanders went looking for "progressive change in unexpected places" in order to show that in Montana and South Dakota and even Utah there actually are liberal activists

---

13. *The Moral Center: How We Can Reclaim Our Country from Die-Hard Extremists, Rogue Corporations, Hollywood Hacks, and Pretend Patriots* (Harcourt, 2006.)

14. *Blue Grit: True Democrats Take Back Politics from the Politicians* (Penguin, 2007).

who are trying to do good things, with very little help or notice from Washington. She writes of liberals who challenge Wal-Mart's employment practices, mount statewide campaigns to allow stem-cell research, and organize protests against the Iraq war. She's not persuasive in arguing that these people and others like them represent a major change that's coming, whether the Democrats are ready for them or not. But her reporting reminds us that while it is the Washington politician's tendency to run away from such fights, it's necessary that there be people out there waging them, and they deserve more attention.[15]

Thomas Schaller, an associate professor at the University of Maryland, suggests a third trajectory, at least for presidential politics: Democrats, he argues, should just ignore the South, where such issues as gays in the military harm them most. *Whistling Past Dixie*[16] makes a strong historical and numerical case that the Democrats can win presidential elections without depending on Southern votes and gratifying Southern mores—trying to appease Southern strictures on personal behavior, he argues, costs them support elsewhere. Schaller's thesis has made him a few enemies among Southern Democratic strategists, such as David "Mudcat" Saunders, the Virginia political consultant who enjoyed a moment of fame a year or two ago as the oracle who would help return the South to the Democratic column. In fact, Democrats made some gains in the region in 2006, notably Webb's win over George Allen and the victory of Mike Beebe, the Democratic candidate for governor in Arkansas. But the large Democratic deficit in the region remains—for example, the eleven states of the Confederacy are represented by sixteen Republican senators and

---

15. I should note that I am quoted once in the book, somewhere between neutrally and unfavorably.

16. *Whistling Past Dixie: How Democrats Can Win Without the South* (Simon and Schuster, 2006.)

six Democrats. In those states' delegations in the House, Republicans hold an 81–50 advantage. Pouring resources into lessening those imbalances, especially while the party is making greater gains in the Mountain West, hardly seems worth the trouble.

In Congress, any far-reaching legislation will face opposition from Senate Republicans, who still have more than enough votes to stop measures from getting to the floor, let alone being passed and sent to the White House. On domestic policy, the best the Democrats can do is hold hearings that will expose the Republican record, approve legislation, at least in committees, and show the public what they'd like to do if they had full power.

By far the most important action the Democrats can take this year is on Iraq. By mid-February, the Senate was at an impasse over a series of non-binding resolutions that condemn in different degrees the President's plan for a surge; but House Democrats were preparing to pass their own resolution. Bush has just sent Congress his proposed defense budget for 2008, a $650 billion bonanza for the defense sector of the economy, of which about $150 billion is earmarked for Iraq and Afghanistan. With public opinion running strongly against the war, the Democrats will be on very safe territory here if they vote to limit military funding for an expansion of the war, whether Bush successfully vetoes legislation or not. Neoconservative critics will bray that the Democrats are betraying the troops and try to argue that "they have painted themselves into a number of corners,"[17] but such views are falling on increasingly deaf ears, even in Washington. The Democrats can't be seen to be causing harm to the troops in Iraq. But short of that, they have plenty of maneuvering room. Finally, unequivocally, and thankfully, most Americans have placed the blame for this fiasco where it belongs.

---

17. The phrase belongs to Noemie Emery, from "Irresolution," *The Weekly Standard*, February 12, 2007.

It will, instead, be up to the presidential candidates to try to sort Iraq out. And they are already doing so. John Edwards calls for an immediate drawdown of 40,000 troops (out of about 140,000). Barack Obama wants a phased redeployment to begin in April, and full withdrawal by March 2008. Hillary Clinton has refused to set a timetable, but she has proposed that a limit be placed on the number of troops in Iraq.[18] Edwards, as if passing from Inferno into Purgatorio, has renounced the sin of his original vote for the war in 2002. Obama has reminded voters that, while merely a state senator in 2002, he nevertheless spoke forcefully (and, as it turns out, presciently) against the war.[19] Clinton has not disavowed her vote but has tap-danced on the narrow stage where antiwar primary voters meet the more hawkish foreign policy establishment, telling a Democratic National Committee audience on February 2 that if she'd been president, she would not have started the war, and that if it's not over by 2009 and she *is* president, she will end it.

These differences among the three leading Democratic presidential candidates—Edwards the most liberal, Obama in the middle, Clinton the most cautious—reflect their candidacies more broadly. Which one wins the nomination will do more, far more than anything Congress does, to suggest how the party will try to create the "lasting Democratic majority" of which Schumer spoke. Clinton will hew closest to Schumer's prescriptions, for example trying to win over parents with talk about the need to reduce the violence of video games, a subject

---

18. A good summation of the leading candidates' positions is found in Tom Hamburger and Janet Hook, "Iraq Plan Divides Democratic Hopefuls," *Los Angeles Times*, February 3, 2007.

19. In a speech he delivered on October 26, 2002, he said in part: "I know that even a successful war against Iraq will require a US occupation of undetermined length, at undetermined cost, with undetermined consequences. I know that an invasion of Iraq without a clear rationale and without strong international support will only fan the flames of the Middle East, and encourage the worst, rather than best, impulses of the Arab world, and strengthen the recruitment arm of al-Qaeda." The entire speech is at en.wikisource.org/wiki/Barack _Obama's_Iraq_Speech.

she has frequently discussed as a senator. Halperin and Harris, in *The Way to Win*, devote fully sixty pages to discussing Clinton's career and speculating how she will run for president. Harris is the editor of the new Web/print publication *The Politico*, and Halperin is the creator of "The Note," ABC.com's influential daily round-up of political coverage. Halperin in particular is a zealous guardian of the conventional wisdom in Washington, and so it's no surprise that the authors speculate darkly that Clinton would probably gravitate more toward "Bush politics" than "Clinton politics" (meaning Bill)—drawing stark ideological distinctions between herself and her opponents in order to vanquish them. But the early evidence suggests that this forecast is completely incorrect and that Clinton will stick to the safe middle ground, advocating smaller-scale initiatives on questions such as health care so as to inoculate herself against the charge of being "liberal."

Instead, it is Edwards who seems intent on making stark distinctions. His will be the most avowedly liberal campaign run by a candidate with a serious chance at the nomination in many years. He clearly believes that a lasting majority can be formed by appealing to the nation's conscience about the need for universal health care and the disgrace of poverty, and he is more forthright about their costs than the other major candidates, saying that he will raise taxes on incomes over $200,000 to finance his health care plan. If he becomes president, Schumer, Clinton, and the Democratic Leadership Council will have to reconsider much of their program.

Obama has announced few clear proposals but he evidently believes it possible to arrive at a Democratic majority not by blurring or accentuating distinctions between different political tendencies but through somehow rendering them anachronistic. The language of civic engagement and asking citizens to be a part of something larger than themselves comes naturally to him. It's my sense that this, more than Clinton's centrism or Edwards's populism (or Schumer's agenda for the Baileys), is the appropriate language for the times. But Obama

has yet to say, in any clearly explained way, just what it is that he will ask citizens to engage themselves in. In his February 10, 2007, announcement speech, he suggested that energy independence, universal health care, and fighting terrorism differently would be priorities. Edwards and Clinton are both well ahead of him when it comes to specifics.

The current moment is without precedent. Until Bush, most Americans had not seen modern conservatism fail them and the country so completely. It is, for now, only a moment. But it's the kind of moment on which realignments are built. It might turn out that Karl Rove has broken the national stalemate after all.

—February 15, 2007

POSTSCRIPT

It is now mid-January 2008. The voters of Iowa and New Hampshire have spoken, and they have performed precisely as anticipated, elevating Barack Obama and Hillary Clinton, allowing John Edwards to hang around for a while longer, and sending everyone else home.

Record numbers have voted. In Iowa, more than 220,000 Democrats showed up to caucus. In New Hampshire, 290,000 voted in the Democratic primary. Both of these totals were larger than the comparable figures on the Republican side, which if nothing else indicates greater enthusiasm among Democratic voters for their candidates.

These are, of course, still minuscule numbers. In November 2004, about 122 million Americans chose their president. Now, a mere half-million have winnowed the Democratic field, in the space of five days, from eight to essentially two. It does, though, appear that Democratic voters at least up through the mega-Tuesday of February 5, when twenty-two states are set to caucus or hold primaries, will be able to participate in deciding whether their nominee will be Clinton or

THE DEMOCRATS

Obama. So voters in more than half the states will have participated in choosing the candidate.

The larger Democratic prospects, as of this writing, still look bright. Republicans seem not to be able to settle on a candidate. Conservatives of my acquaintance are convinced that the Republicans will be wiped out in November at both the presidential and congressional levels. They are probably exaggerating, and Democrats, who will be sending either an African-American man or the country's most polarizing woman politician into battle bearing their standard, should maintain caution. But all things considered, the political landscape of 2008 presents the Democratic Party with an opportunity it has not had in a very, very long time: for a Democratic president and a Democratic Congress, with a mandate to make progressive change. So the question is, what would they make of such an opportunity?

Since Schumer and Emmanuel and Reed wrote their books, and over the course of the early months of the presidential election, it is fair to say that both Clinton and Obama have embraced agendas somewhat more far-reaching than the ones recommended by those authors. Both candidates have advocated policies that don't merely cater to the self-interest of middle-class voters but that are based on some vision of a larger common good, whether they involve plans for universal health care or a wide-ranging network of energy proposals to fight global warming. Both candidates have sounded skeptical notes about free trade. Both pledge phased withdrawal from Iraq. In the intraparty fight between liberals and centrists, liberals have for now gained the upper hand.

But an upper hand during a primary campaign, when candidates are trying to pander to core constituencies, doesn't necessarily translate into dominance in an administration. Clinton's preternatural caution and Obama's instinct to find middle ground suggest that both would pick their spots carefully, perhaps too carefully. Much will hinge on the prosaic but very concrete question of how large a

working majority a Democratic president will have. It seems a safe assumption that the party's majority in the House will hold at the current thirty-three seats or perhaps even expand somewhat. Eyes will be on the Senate, where the Republican minority blocked the progress of Democratic legislation on dozens of occasions in 2007. If the Democrats manage to pick up five seats, the combination of those gains and the possible willingness under the new circumstances of the remaining handful of moderate Republicans to buck their leadership and reach compromise with Democrats should produce enough of a genuine working majority to accomplish at least some progressive goals.

Even under the most optimistic projection, change will come slowly, too slowly to suit an impatient age. But the opportunity may exist to change American political life not for the next four years but the next forty.

—January 18, 2008

# 9

## THE REPUBLICANS

### Michael Tomasky

AS THE VOTING begins in earnest, what are we to make of the Republican candidates? That the "conservative base" is dissatisfied with the GOP field is probably the single most common observation of this presidential campaign season. The second most common observation is probably that the Republican candidate, whoever it turns out to be, is doomed to defeat. *National Review* ran a recent cover story positing not only that the GOP is likely to lose the presidency in 2008, but that the loss may mark the beginning of a long period of wandering in the wilderness as the party gropes to redefine itself after George W. Bush's calamitous tenure. Ramesh Ponnuru and Richard Lowry write:

> Conservatives tend to blame their travails on Republican politicians' missteps and especially on their inability to communicate. But the public's unhappiness with Republicans goes much deeper than any such explanation. A mishandled war, coupled with intellectual exhaustion on the domestic front, has soured the public on them. It is not just the politicians but conservative voters themselves who are out of touch with the public, stuck in the glory days of the 1980s and not thinking nearly enough about how to make their principles relevant to the concerns

of today. Unforeseen events could yet change the political environment radically. As it stands, Republicans are sleep-walking into catastrophe.[1]

What would be a rational Republican response to this grim state of affairs? Given both the apparent ideological heterogeneity of the candidates and the soul-searching taking place even in the pages of *National Review* about how badly conservatism has failed the country, one might think that the GOP in 2008 would disclaim at least some of its current radical conservative positions and inch back toward the political center.

David Frum, the conservative analyst who formerly wrote speeches for Bush, proposes something along these lines (although he prefers calling it conservatism updated for the twenty-first century rather than centrism) in *Comeback*.[2] To help the GOP recover from its present shabby state, for example, Frum preaches a "Green Conservatism" in which the GOP fights the Democrats for the allegiance of environmentally minded voters, going so far as to endorse a carbon tax. He also advocates a conservatism for the middle class that actually wants to do something about the problem of uninsured middle-class Americans. He even calls for a conservatism that respects the rights of prisoners, including "conjugal visits" and "enjoyable food." He combines these with newfangled defenses of traditional conservative positions —for example, a softer opposition to abortion that emphasizes "education and persuasion rather than coercion, changes in attitudes and beliefs rather than changes in law and public policy." More than once while reading *Comeback*, I nodded, thinking that the GOP could do worse than to listen to him. In urging a new course, he joins other conservative writers like Ross Douthat and Reihan Salam, who

---

1. "The Grim Truth," *National Review*, November 19, 2007.

2. *Comeback: Conservatism That Can Win Again* (Doubleday, 2008).

argued in *The Weekly Standard* in 2005 for a "Sam's Club Conservatism" that makes economic appeals to working-class voters.

Whatever Frum may hope for, however, we have to deal with actually existing Republicanism, as it is being played out in the current race. And that Republicanism is quite the opposite: on nearly every issue, the major candidates have run hard to the right, exceptions (John McCain on immigration) being vastly outnumbered by the rule. All of the major candidates agree, among other things, on policy toward Iraq and Iran, on judicial appointments, and on low taxes for the well-off.

Conventional wisdom would assert that they have done so simply to pander to Republican primary voters, and that the nominee will move toward the center for the general election. He may well do so as a matter of political calculation. Just one or two slightly heterodox positions that reduce well to journalistic shorthand—on education, or, as Frum suggests, on the environment—should do the trick.

But the important question is not how the nominee will position himself next fall. Think, after all, about Bush's talk of "compassionate conservatism" in 2000 and about how the national press fell for it. The important question is how he will govern should he win. And the generally ignored story of this race so far is that in truth, dramatic ideological change among the Republicans is highly unlikely. Despite Bush's failures and the discrediting of conservative governance, there is every chance that the next Republican president, should the party's nominee prevail next year, will be just as conservative as Bush has been—perhaps even more so.

How could this be? The explanation is fairly simple. It has little to do with the out-of-touch politicians and conservative voters Ponnuru and Lowry cite and reflects instead the central hard truth about the components of the Republican Party today. That is, the party is still in the hands of three main interests: neoconservatives; theoconservatives, i.e., the groups of the religious right; and radical anti-

taxers, clustered around such organizations as the Club for Growth and Grover Norquist's Americans for Tax Reform. Each of these groups dominates party policy in its area of interest—the neocons in foreign policy, the theocons in social policy, and the anti-taxers on fiscal and regulatory issues.[3] Each has led the Bush administration to undertake a high-profile failure: the theocons orchestrated the disastrous Terri Schiavo crusade, which put off many moderate Americans; the radical anti-taxers pushed for the failed Social Security privatization initiative; and the neocons, of course, wanted to invade Iraq.

Three failures, and there are more like them. And yet, so far as the internal dynamics of the Republican Party are concerned, they have been failures without serious consequence, because there are no strong countervailing Republican forces to present an opposite view or argue a different set of policies and principles.

The two major American political parties have always been amalgams of factions, especially the Democratic Party, from its early tensions between Jacksonian frontier populists and Adams-descended Northern reformers up through the late-nineteenth-century disputes between the mercantilist "Bourbon Democrats" and the prairie populists led by William Jennings Bryan. Then came the uneasy New Deal coalition of Northern liberals and Southern segregationists, and finally, in our time, the sometimes bitter feuds between liberals and centrists. The Republican Party's history is slightly less convulsive, partly because its initial factions such as Whigs and Free-Soilers found unity under Abraham Lincoln on the central question of slavery. But in time the

---

3. Big business, the traditional linchpin of the GOP, is more divided this year than at any time in recent memory. One of many representative pieces of evidence is Jeanne Cummings, "Business Abandons GOP for Democrats," *The Politico*, October 15, 2007. Cummings reported that "all 10 of the top-giving industries tracked by the Center for Responsive Politics, a nonpartisan money and politics watchdog group, are now donating more cash to Democrats than Republicans." Only the oil and gas sector held firm for the GOP. (On December 11, 2007, *National Review* endorsed Mitt Romney on the grounds that the editors find him most likely to unite and please precisely these three constituencies.)

Republican coalition came to include both staunchly pro-business and trust-busting interests; nearer our own era, there was also room enough within the party for domestic conservatives and moderates, supporters and foes of the New Deal, and foreign policy internationalists and isolationists.

Today's Republican Party is different. It is essentially a faction: the conservative movement, which consists of the various branches described above, each with its different priorities. (We may lately add a fourth offshoot, the nativist anti-immigrant tendency, which embarrassed Bush last spring when it blocked the reasonable and comprehensive immigration bill the President supported.) Those branches, which of course overlap, are not sharply at odds with one another over fundamental questions, as the Democrats' factions are on, say, trade, and where they disagree, they tend not to air those disagreements publicly, especially at election time.[4] There are a handful of vestigial Republican moderates; but they have no national power at all. The man who might have been able to change the party, the governor of the nation's largest state, cannot by accident of birth run for president, so he has gone as far as he can. In Congress, Republicans who are the least bit out of step with the goals of the conservative movement, people who in a different party might have made attractive national candidates (most notably Nebraska Senator Chuck Hagel), are simply jumping ship and retiring, unable any longer to fight the obvious truth that the Republican Party and the conservative movement are one and the same.

The disarray following a loss next year might well embolden the moderate forces to stage a comeback. But suppose the Republican nominee wins next November, a possibility that is not as far-fetched as it may seem, particularly if some development in the Middle East

---

4. There was some dissent on Iraq. Norquist, for example, had misgivings about the war from early on but did not make them public until after Bush won reelection.

or a national security threat were used to scare voters. No matter what the polls say today, a campaign built around scaring Americans into thinking that the Democrat will not protect them is one that always stands a chance of working, especially if that Democrat is a black man or a woman. Should that happen, there is no credible reason to believe that the neocons, theocons, and anti-taxers will hold any less power in the new administration than they have in Bush's.

On foreign policy, despite the Iraq war, the neoconservatives still hold tremendous sway in GOP circles. Jacob Heilbrunn, a former *New Republic* writer who has written incisively about the movement over the years, explains why in *They Knew They Were Right*,[5] his excellent new history of neoconservatism. Heilbrunn adroitly surveys the movement's history, from the Trotskyist alcoves of the City College cafeteria up to the present day. With respect to the future, he argues that the neocons' main potential competitors, the foreign policy realists, have not prepared for long-term battle the way the neocons have:

> So it will take an insurgency inside the GOP itself to dislodge the neoconservatives. But whether the old guard in the GOP has the mettle for that battle is dubious. There has been no real attempt to create new generations of realists to replace the Scowcrofts and Bakers and Schlesingers. The contrast between the Nixon Center event honoring Brent Scowcroft in 2006 and the [American Enterprise Institute] dinner for Bernard Lewis was striking. At the former, elderly veterans of the Nixon, Ford, and Bush administrations reminisced about their glory days.... Meanwhile, at the AEI dinner, none of the neoconservatives displayed much doubt about their own influence. *Slate*'s Jacob Weisberg, for example, was dumbfounded by neoconservative serenity....

---

5. *They Knew They Were Right: The Rise of the Neocons* (Doubleday, 2008).

The extent to which the major Republican candidates, with the partial exception of Mike Huckabee, have backed the neocon worldview is striking. Exhibit A is of course Rudy Giuliani. The former mayor has organized his campaign around the fight against terrorism and to that end has assembled a hard-line foreign policy team led by Yale professor Charles Hill, a noted neoconservative and member of the Project for a New American Century (PNAC), the group that pressed Bush to invade Iraq after September 11. (Nine days after the attacks, Hill signed a PNAC letter arguing that refusal to invade Iraq "will constitute an early and perhaps decisive surrender in the war on international terrorism."[6]) Norman Podhoretz, who has a prominent spot on the Giuliani team, is still agitating for war with Iran, even after the early December 2007 release of the National Intelligence Estimate that demolished any rationale for such a strike. Podhoretz writes of his "dark suspicions" that the intelligence community was both seeking to undermine Bush and rushing to judgment on the basis of scant evidence.[7]

Giuliani has written, or at least put his name to, a bromide-laden piece in the September–October 2007 issue of *Foreign Affairs*—the kind of grand foreign policy statement that presidential aspirants feel obliged to make. The essay, which opens with the sentence "We are all members of the 9/11 generation," embraces the basic neocon outlook that we are locked in a struggle to the death with forces of "Islamic fascism" whose adherents hate us for our freedoms, and capitalizes phrases like "the Terrorists' War on Us" (twice in the first seven paragraphs). On Iraq, Giuliani elsewhere says that "I think we should give our troops a chance to succeed in Iraq. Our goal in Iraq is victory."

McCain has positioned himself as one of the Senate's leading hawks on Iraq, going out of his way to heap abuse on the Baker-

---

6. See www.newamericancentury.org/Bushletter.htm.

7. From Podhoretz's blog on *Commentary*'s Web site; see www.commentary magazine.com/blogs/index.php/podhoretz/1474.

Hamilton Iraq Study Group report a year ago, even before Bush made up his mind to reject its findings. In a recent debate, he said that in Iraq "we are succeeding.... Now we have a successful strategy. We can succeed. We will succeed." His foreign policy team is somewhat more diverse than Giuliani's (he says he talks to a few realists, such as Scowcroft), but it, too, includes many prominent neocons: William Kristol, Robert Kagan, and Max Boot; Gary Schmitt of the American Enterprise Institute; and Randy Scheunemann, a former director of PNAC who helped found the Committee for the Liberation of Iraq, an advocacy group that pushed for war against Iraq after September 11.

Mitt Romney's advisers on foreign policy are less well known. They include Dan Senor, the former spokesman of the Coalition Provisional Authority in Iraq, and longtime CIA analyst Cofer Black, the point man for the US government's counterterrorism policy during Bush's first term, and now the vice-chair of Blackwater USA, the largest of the State Department's "private security" contractors in Iraq. One of Romney's more memorable utterances from this campaign was his vow to "double Guantánamo," made in May 2007 at a forum when he was asked about interrogation techniques for terror suspects.

Mike Huckabee, until recently not considered a serious candidate, didn't have the money in early 2007 to assemble any such team. That may be one reason why he has departed somewhat from the prevailing views. Huckabee's major foreign policy statement came in an essay in the January–February 2008 issue of *Foreign Affairs*. The article made headlines when it was released in mid-December for its assertion that the Bush administration was guilty of an "arrogant bunker mentality" in dealing with the world. Some Bush foes praised Huckabee's forthrightness, while other candidates, especially Romney, attacked him.

But the policies he describes would represent less of a departure from Bush foreign policy than his attention-getting phrase suggests. He is far more critical of Pakistan and President Pervez Musharraf than most neoconservatives, and he places somewhat more emphasis

on negotiations with Iran than do Bush or Huckabee's opponents. But he supports the administration's sanctions against Iran. He endorses the same stay-the-course position on Iraq. And he sees the battle against terrorism in the same kind of cultural terms, although his rhetoric of choice is Southern Baptist rather than chastened leftist (i.e., the neocons): "America's culture of life stands in stark contrast to the jihadists' culture of death."[8]

As a second-tier candidate, Huckabee was not expected to flash any great expertise on foreign policy, and he apparently didn't make much of an effort to acquire it. A full day after the Iran NIE was released, Huckabee had to admit to a reporter that he hadn't heard of it.[9] If Huckabee continues to be one of the top candidates, we should pay attention to his foreign policy pronouncements. It's a good bet that he will undergo some crash tutorials and start to sound more like Giuliani and McCain.

The theoconservatives are thought to be on the defensive this election cycle, with their grip on the GOP loosening. In some superficial ways this is true. There is no candidate who passes every one of their basic litmus test issues, and, if Rudy Giuliani wins the nomination, the party will have selected a pro-choice nominee for the first time since 1976. Still, where is the countervailing force to the religious right in the party? As with the neocons, there is none. (Frances FitzGerald and other writers have observed a more liberal trend among some of the large evangelical churches; but right-wing evangelicals continue to dominate among Republicans.) There are also organizations like the Ripon Society, which tries to press moderate social programs within the party, and there are nominal blocs of libertarians, but these groups are vastly outspent and outnumbered.

---

8. "America's Priorities in the War on Terror," *Foreign Affairs*, January/February 2008.

9. See Rick Pearson, "Huckabee Says He's Unfamiliar with Intel Report," *Chicago Tribune*, December 4, 2007.

The religious right—in the form of its umbrella organization the Arlington Group, formed in 2002—is certainly split and unenthusiastic about the presidential candidates. Pat Robertson has endorsed Giuliani; Richard Land, the head of the Southern Baptist Convention, has said he could never vote for Giuliani and would consider backing a third-party candidate if Giuliani is nominated. So the unanimity on Bush's behalf we saw in 2000 and in 2004 will likely be gone. But as far as policy is concerned, the Christian right has only one overriding goal: a promise from candidates that they'll appoint "strict constructionist" judges. And every one of the candidates, Giuliani included, has made that promise resoundingly and repeatedly, in public and presumably in private. As recently as November 2007, Giuliani told the conservative Federalist Society that "we need judges who embrace originalism" and vowed that he would appoint justices in the mold of Antonin Scalia and Clarence Thomas.[10]

That, above all, is what the Christian right needs to hear. It is well worth remembering that when the next president is sworn in, John Paul Stevens will be three months shy of his eighty-ninth birthday. It seems unlikely that he would be able to outlast a Giuliani or Romney or Huckabee or McCain presidency. One more judge like John Roberts or Samuel Alito will mean not only the probable end of *Roe* v. *Wade* but of affirmative action (sharply curtailed already), efforts at school desegregation (school systems have resegregated to a surprising extent in recent years), and many other progressive social goals. All of the four major Republican candidates have vowed to see to these outcomes. Paradoxically, the personally pro-choice Giuliani, if elected, could go down in history as a hero to the Christian right—the president who finally ended *Roe*—in a way that even Ronald Reagan has not.

---

10. See David G. Savage, "Giuliani Says He'd Pick Conservative Justices," *Los Angeles Times*, November 17, 2007.

The candidates' pledges about judges highlight an important point. Lack of enthusiasm is not the same thing as lack of power, and the religious right still has power in the nominating process. Consider Mitt Romney's recent speech on religion. In the speech, billed as Romney's "JFK moment" because he would squarely address issues raised by his Mormon faith just as Kennedy famously did with regard to Catholicism, Romney promised that he would uphold the Constitution, not Latter Day Saints doctrine. But he also seemed to embrace a test for Americanism that stipulated some kind of religious belief, ignoring the long-held principles, to which even George Bush has paid rhetorical heed, that religious freedom includes the freedom not to believe and that nonbelievers can be good Americans, too. Romney found his mark: while the speech registered as perfunctory or disappointing in most mainstream circles, James Dobson, the founder of Focus on the Family, called it "magnificent," "passionate," and "inspirational." (Dobson has not yet endorsed a candidate.)

The third leg of the conservative movement is in many ways the most important and comprehensive: all conservatives agree on less government, lower taxes, and less regulation. And all the candidates have pledged to support these goals.

Frum reminds us that in the real world, the salience of tax-cutting as an issue has been steadily eroding in recent years:

> When Republicans speak of "tax cuts," they mean "income tax cuts." Yet after almost three decades of income-tax cutting, most Americans no longer pay very much income tax. In fact, four out of five taxpayers now pay more in payroll taxes than federal income taxes. Some 29 million income-earning American households pay no income tax at all. By contrast, the notorious top 1 percent of taxpayers pay well over one-third of all US income taxes. The top 1 percent may make a disproportionate amount of money. But they still cast only 1 percent of the votes.

One can quibble that Frum's math is probably slightly off since higher-income citizens are more likely to vote than poor people. But he is correct that for most Americans there simply isn't much more income tax to cut, and that poll respondents repeatedly prefer either deficit reduction or particular types of public investment, such as health care.

But the major Republican candidates give no sign that it may be time to shift to a different set of priorities. They all emphasize tax-cutting and deregulation as the centerpieces of their economic policies, including now McCain, who had opposed the Bush tax cuts in 2001 and 2003. Indeed, one gets little indication from their speeches and platforms that serious domestic needs even exist. In August, for example, Giuliani released a health care plan whose main feature is tax exclusions of up to $7,500 per person and $15,000 per family that buys a health care plan. In order to help a family buy insurance, he proposed $15,000 of its income would not be taxed. But in reality, most uninsured families would derive little or no benefit from this plan because their incomes are already below the taxable level regardless of whether they are taking the exclusion. Even for wealthier households whose tax burdens would be reduced, the savings would certainly not come close to the $10,000 to $12,000 per year that most households would have to pay for family coverage.

So what is the purpose of Giuliani's plan? The journalist Ezra Klein characterized it with asperity, and accuracy:

> Rudy Giuliani doesn't have a health care plan. What he has is a pretext with which to attack the Democrats. Indeed, just about all you need to know about Giuliani's thoughtfulness on the issue can be summed up by the following: In the speech introducing and detailing his new health care proposal, Giuliani refers to the "Democrats" six times. "Single-payer" is said eight

times. "Socialized medicine," or some variant thereof, makes nine appearances. "Uninsured" is never uttered—not once.[11]

The reason Giuliani cannot release a health care plan that makes a genuine attempt at insuring the uninsured is not resistance from "politicians" and "conservative voters," as Ponnuru and Lowry claim. He cannot do so because the important interest groups—such as the Club for Growth—that influence Republican fiscal policy would write him off, and in fact oppose him vehemently, if he tried to.

As an example of courageous heterodoxy on economic matters, some have pointed to Huckabee, whose record as governor of Arkansas, when he increased some taxes and spending on education, did indeed place him at loggerheads with the Club for Growth, which is distrustful of his record. But this is fantasy. Huckabee—as he hastens to point out when pressed on this matter—was compelled by state law to balance the budget (state governments can't run deficits or print money), and he was under court order to increase spending on education.

For the nation as a whole, Huckabee proposes a regressive and onerous national sales tax. Called, with the usual spin, the "fair tax," Huckabee's tax plan would add about 30 percent (by conservative estimates) to the purchase price of durable goods, many household items, and even automobiles.[12] It is arguably the most regressive tax plan put forward by any candidate. It comes as no surprise that despite the Club for Growth's remonstrations, Huckabee is in good standing with Americans for Tax Reform, whose famous "pledge" not to raise taxes under any circumstances he has agreed to.

---

11. See Ezra Klein, "A Man with a (Non-) Plan," *The American Prospect* on-line, August 2, 2007.

12. The Huckabee campaign has described the national sales tax, which would amount to $30 on a $100 purchase, as a 23 percent tax, but the figure is misleading, since it is based on the new total price—$30 is 23 percent of $130—rather than on the original purchase amount that is being taxed. In fact, the additional tax would be equal to 30 percent of the purchase's pre-tax value of $100.

It is tempting to think that the Bush years have represented an apotheosis of conservatism, and that a future Republican administration would surely bring a kind of Thermidorean adjustment. It is also the case, obviously, that none of these men is George W. Bush and that each of them, as president, might at least be less stubborn, more interested in the details of policy, and less hostile to empirical evidence that does not support his preconceived notions.

But at the same time, one must remember that as far as movement conservatives are concerned, Bush has been something of a disappointment, and vast chunks of their plan for the country remain unrealized. The neocons will not quit wanting a preemptive strike against Iran, something the December NIE has seemingly ruled out for the rest of Bush's term; they will welcome a fresh opportunity to push their case with an administration the public has not yet learned to distrust. The theocons still want *Roe* overturned, along with some other Warren Court precedents (watch, if the next president is a Republican, for a fresh assault on Warren-era decisions on criminal and civil procedure, for example *Miranda* v. *Arizona*). And for the radical anti-taxers' tastes, the federal government is still far too large, its regulations far too numerous, and income tax and capital gains tax rates, even at their already reduced levels, far too high, not to mention the continued existence of that pesky Social Security system.

The Republican nominee, once he is named next spring, will undoubtedly tack toward the center during the general election campaign. But again, the important question is how he would govern. Presidents respond to the constituencies that put them in office, and a Republican president elected in 2008 will have been put in office by the factions that control his party. There is no reason to expect that he will defy those factions. Let us hope that in the long run, the Republicans outside them will decide to challenge their power.

—December 19, 2007

# 10

## HISTORY AND NATIONAL STUPIDITY

### *Arthur Schlesinger Jr.*

HISTORY IS NOT self-executing. You do not put a coin in the slot and have history come out. For the past is a chaos of events and personalities into which we cannot penetrate. It is beyond retrieval and it is beyond reconstruction. All historians know this in their souls. "There is no such thing as human history," one historian has told the New-York Historical Society.

> Nothing can be more profoundly, sadly true. The annals of mankind have never been written, never can be written; nor would it be within human capacity to read them if they were written. We have a leaf or two from the great book of human fate as it flutters in the stormwinds ever sweeping across the earth. We decipher them as we best can with purblind eyes, and endeavor to learn their mystery as we float along to the abyss; but it is all confused babble, hieroglyphics of which the key is lost.

The scholar who uttered these stark postmodernist sentiments was John Lothrop Motley, the great nineteenth-century historian of the Netherlands, speaking to the New-York Historical Society in December 1868.

All historians are prisoners of their own experience and servitors to their own prepossessions. We are all entrapped in the egocentric predicament. We bring to history the preconceptions of our personality and the preoccupations of our age. We cannot seize on ultimate and absolute truths. "Purely objective truth," said William James, "is nowhere to be found. . . . The trail of the human serpent is thus over everything."

So the historian is committed to a doomed enterprise—the quest for an unattainable objectivity. Yet it is an enterprise we happily pursue, because of the thrill of the hunt, because exploring the past is such fun, because of the intellectual challenges involved, because a nation needs to know its own history (or so we historians like to think).

As I have suggested elsewhere, history is to the nation as memory is to the individual. As a person deprived of memory becomes disoriented and lost, not knowing where he has been or where he is going, so a nation denied a conception of its past will be disabled in dealing with its present and its future.

But conceptions of the past are far from stable. They are perennially revised by the urgencies of the present. When new urgencies arise in our own times and lives, the historian's spotlight shifts, probing now into the shadows, throwing into sharp relief things that were always there but that earlier historians had carelessly excised from the collective memory. New voices ring out of the historical darkness and demand attention.

One has only to note how in the last half-century the women's rights movement and the civil rights movement have reformulated and renewed American history. Thus the present incessantly recreates, reinvents, the past. In this sense, all history, as Benedetto Croce said, is contemporary history. It is these permutations of consciousness that make history so endlessly fascinating an intellectual adventure. "The one duty we owe to history," said Oscar Wilde, "is to rewrite it."

J. R. Seeley was a nineteenth-century Victorian and his definition of history as "past politics" ruled the curriculum for a while. Then came social history and the consequent discomfiture of political and intellectual history. Social history diverted the spotlight to minorities, hitherto neglected in standard historical works. When I went to college in the 1930s, the study of slavery was still influenced by the writings of Ulrich B. Phillips, who took an indulgent view of it. Discussion of the causes of the Civil War was dominated by the denial of James G. Randall and Avery Craven, and for that matter Charles A. Beard, that the war was inevitable and slavery its cause. Instead, these historians contended, a "blundering generation," driven by fanaticism, especially by the fanaticism of the abolitionists, had transformed a "repressive conflict" into a "needless war." As for Reconstruction, the view of W. A. Dunning and Claude Bowers was that the white South had to be rescued from the barbarous freed slaves and their villainous Yankee carpetbagger allies.

Ulrich Phillips on slavery and James Randall and Avery Craven on the causes of the Civil War have long since been discarded in the teaching of American history. As for Dunning and Bowers on Reconstruction, I recall an incident that shows how new pressures overrule old perspectives. In June 1963, when Governor George Wallace tried to block the admission of two black students to the University of Alabama, President Kennedy sent in the National Guard to secure their admission. That night he went on television to explain his action. Racial equality, Kennedy said, was "a moral issue...as old as the Scriptures and...as clear as the American Constitution." That same night in Mississippi Medgar Evers, the director of the state NAACP, was murdered.

The next week the President invited Medgar Evers's widow and their children to the White House and he asked me to sit in on their meeting. They were an exceptionally attractive family. When they left, I said to President Kennedy, "What a terrible business." Kennedy

said sadly, "Yes. I don't understand the South. I'm coming to believe that [the vehemently anti-Southern abolitionist] Thaddeus Stevens was right. I had always been taught to regard him as a man of vicious bias. But when I see this sort of thing, I begin to wonder how else you can treat them [i.e., the Southern racists]." The change from the Dunning and Bowers school that had taught Kennedy to the work of Eric Foner was nothing less than a revolution in historians' handling of Reconstruction.

Sean Wilentz and his *Rise of American Democracy: Jefferson to Lincoln* has a penetrating account of the causes of the Civil War. He has also most generous remarks about my book *The Age of Jackson*. The special contribution of *The Age of Jackson* was, I suppose, to shift the argument from section to class. *The Age of Jackson* was written more than sixty years ago in another America, and reflected FDR's struggles to democratize American capitalism. I was an ardent young New Dealer, and I sought precedents in American history for the problems that faced FDR.

In advancing my interpretation, I was conditioned by the passions of my era. Conservatives in the angry Thirties used to fulminate against the New Deal as "un-American." I wanted to show that far from importing foreign ideas, FDR was acting in a robust American spirit and tradition. Jackson's war against Nicholas Biddle and the Second Bank of the United States thus provided a thoroughly American precedent for the battles that FDR waged against the "economic royalists" of his (and my) day.

FDR saw it this way too. Years later, I came upon a letter he had written to Colonel Edward M. House, Woodrow Wilson's *homme de confiance*, in November 1933. "The real truth of the matter," Roosevelt told House,

> is, as you and I know, that a financial element in the larger centers has owned the Government ever since the days of Andrew

Jackson—and I am not wholly excepting the Administration of W. W. The country is going through a repetition of Jackson's fight with the Bank of the United States—only on a far bigger and broader basis.

Jackson and Roosevelt, it appeared, had much the same coalition of supporters—farmers, workingmen, intellectuals, the poor—and much the same coalition of adversaries—bankers, merchants, manufacturers, and the rich. There was consequently a striking parallel between the 1830s and the 1930s in politics, and there was striking parallelism in the basic issue of power—the struggle for control of the state between organized money and the rest of society. I was hopelessly absorbed in the dilemmas of democratic capitalism made vivid for my generation by FDR and the New Deal, and I underplayed and ignored other aspects of the Age of Jackson. The predicament of slaves, of the red man and the "trail of tears"—the forcible removal of the Cherokees and other Indians from Georgia to the far frontier—and the restricted opportunities for women of the period (save for Peggy Eaton, the wife of John Eaton, Jackson's secretary of war, a woman who in 1920s style rebelled against convention with Jackson's support) were shamefully out of my mind.

Sean Wilentz has done what I should have done in his brilliant, powerful work *The Rise of American Democracy*. He has given slavery and the Indians their proper place in the Age of Jackson, and he describes Jackson's failures to deal with both. The perspective of 2000 is bound to be different from the perspective of 1940. And the perspective of 2060 is bound to be different from the perspective of 2000—and I trust Sean will still be around.

There remains Motley's despair over the knowability of the past. This despair has been recently reinforced by what has become known as the linguistic turn. Motley's doubts reappear, this time decked out with postmodernist jargon of deconstruction, discourse analysis,

intertextuality, and narratology. All history is seen in this light as the continuation of ideology by other means, as the projection and manipulation of relationships of domination and oppression. Some philosophers of history would even abolish, or at least attenuate, the distinction between the stories historians tell and other forms of storytelling.

Of course most working historians repudiate the idea that there is no real difference between history and fiction. For historians, observes the British Marxist scholar Eric Hobsbawm, a dear friend of mine for nearly seventy years, "even for the most militantly antipositivist ones among us, the ability to distinguish between the two is absolutely fundamental. We cannot invent our facts. Either Elvis Presley is dead or he isn't." In view of the doubts about Elvis's death frequently expressed in supermarket tabloids, we can perhaps amend Hobsbawm's statement by substituting the name of someone safely dead, like Napoleon. For there is an external reality that exists independently of our representations. We can appreciate Motley's despair over penetrating that reality and getting history right. The hieroglyphics have no key. But history is not an illusion or a fiction or a myth. "True as the present *is*," said William James, "the past *was* also."

I am impressed these days by the apparent popularity of the History Channel on television. I hope that this expresses a growing historical consciousness among our people. For we are the world's dominant power, and I believe that history is a moral necessity for a nation possessed of overweening power. History verifies John F. Kennedy's proposition in the first year of his presidency, when he said:

> We must face the fact that the United States is neither omnipotent or omniscient—that we are only 6 percent of the world's population—that we cannot impose our will upon the other 94 percent of mankind—that we cannot right every wrong or

reverse each adversity—and that therefore there cannot be an American solution to every world problem.

History is the best antidote to illusions of omnipotence and omniscience. It should forever remind us of the limitations of our passing perspectives. It should strengthen us to resist the pressure to convert momentary interests into moral absolutes. It should lead us to a profound and chastening sense of our frailty as human beings—to a recognition of the fact, so often and so sadly demonstrated, that the future will outwit all our certitudes and that the possibilities of history are far richer and more various than the human intellect is likely to conceive.

A nation informed by a vivid understanding of the ironies of history is, I believe, best equipped to live with the temptations and tragedy of power. Since we are condemned as a nation to be a superpower, let a growing sense of history temper and civilize our use of that power.

Sometimes, when I am particularly depressed, I ascribe our behavior to stupidity—the stupidity of our leadership, the stupidity of our culture. Thirty years ago we suffered military defeat—fighting an unwinnable war against a country about which we knew nothing and in which we had no vital interests at stake. Vietnam was bad enough, but to repeat the same experiment thirty years later in Iraq is a strong argument for a case of national stupidity.

In the meantime, let a thousand historical flowers bloom. History is never a closed book or a final verdict. It is always in the making. Let historians not forsake the quest for knowledge, however tricky and full of problems that quest may be, in the interests of an ideology, a nation, a race, a sex, or a cause. The great strength of the practice of history in a free society is its capacity for self-correction.

This is the endless fascination of historical writing: the search to reconstruct what went before, a quest illuminated by those ever-

changing prisms that continually place old questions in a new light. As the great Dutch historian Pieter Geyl was fond of saying, "History is indeed an argument without end." That, I believe, is why we love it so much.

# Notes on the Contributors

MARK DANNER is the author of *The Massacre at El Mozote: A Parable of the Cold War* (1994), *The Road to Illegitimacy: One Reporter's Travels Through the 2000 Florida Recount* (2003), *Torture and Truth: America, Abu Ghraib, and the War on Terror* (2004), and *The Secret Way to War: The Downing Street Memo and the Iraq War's Buried History* (2006). He is Professor of Journalism at the University of California, Berkeley, and Henry R. Luce Professor of Human Rights and Journalism and James Clarke Chace Professor of Foreign Affairs, Politics, and the Humanities at Bard College. "'The Moment Has Come to Get Rid of Saddam'" originally appeared in *The New York Review* of November 8, 2007.

JOAN DIDION's books include *The Year of Magical Thinking* (2005) and *We Tell Ourselves Stories in Order to Live: Collected Nonfiction* (2006). "Cheney: The Fatal Touch" originally appeared in *The New York Review* of October 5, 2006.

JONATHAN FREEDLAND is an editorial-page columnist for *The Guardian*. He is the author of *Bring Home the Revolution: The Case for a British Republic* (1999). "Bush's Amazing Achievement" originally appeared in *The New York Review* of June 14, 2007.

PETER GALBRAITH is a former US ambassador to Croatia and the author of *The End of Iraq: How American Incompetence Created a War Without End* (2006) and *Unintended Consequences* (2008). "The Victor" originally appeared in *The New York Review* of October 11, 2007.

JOSEPH LELYVELD is a former editor and correspondent of *The New York Times*. He is the author of *Omaha Blues: A Memory Loop* (2005). "No Exit" originally appeared in *The New York Review* of February 15, 2007.

JONATHAN RABAN's books include *Bad Land: An American Romance* (1996), *Passage to Juneau: A Sea and Its Meanings* (1999), *Waxwings* (2003), *Surveillance* (2006), and *My Holy War: Dispatches from the Home Front* (2006). "Cracks in the House of Rove" originally appeared in *The New York Review* of April 12, 2007.

FRANK RICH is a columnist for *The New York Times* and the author of *The Greatest Story Ever Sold: The Decline and Fall of Truth from 9/11 to Katrina* (2006). "Ideas for Democrats" originally appeared in *The New York Review* of October 19, 2006.

ARTHUR SCHLESINGER JR. (1917–2007) served as an adviser to Presidents Kennedy and Johnson. He was the author of numerous books on American history, including *The Age of Jackson* and the three-volume *The Age of Roosevelt*. "History and National Stupidity" originally appeared in *The New York Review* of April 27, 2006.

ROBERT B. SILVERS is cofounder and editor of *The New York Review of Books*. He is the editor of *Hidden Histories of Science* and *Five Performing Arts*, and co-editor of *The Legacy of Isaiah Berlin*, *Striking Terror: America's New War*, and *India: A Mosaic*.

MICHAEL TOMASKY is the editor of Guardian America, *The Guardian*'s American Web site. "The Democrats" originally appeared in *The New York Review* of March 15, 2007. "The Republicans" originally appeared in *The New York Review* of January 17, 2008, under the title "They'd Rather Be Right."